# THE 101 BEST

# GRAPHIC NOVELS

# THE 101 BEST GRAPHIC NOVELS

## Stephen Weiner

NANTIER · BEALL · MINOUSTCHINE
Publishing inc.
new york

24.95

*The 101 Best Graphic Novels* ©2005 Stephen Weiner
Covers and artwork © their respective owners
Editor: Keith R. A. DeCandido
Foreword ©1996 Neil Gaiman
Book and Cover Design by Chris Shadoian
Cover artwork ©2005 Will Eisner


Hardcover Edition
ISBN-10: 1-56163-443-3
ISBN-13: 978-1-56163-443-9

Paperback Edition
ISBN-10: 1-56163-444-1
ISBN-13: 978-1-56163-444-6


Library of Congress control number: 2005932866

This book is
for Rachel

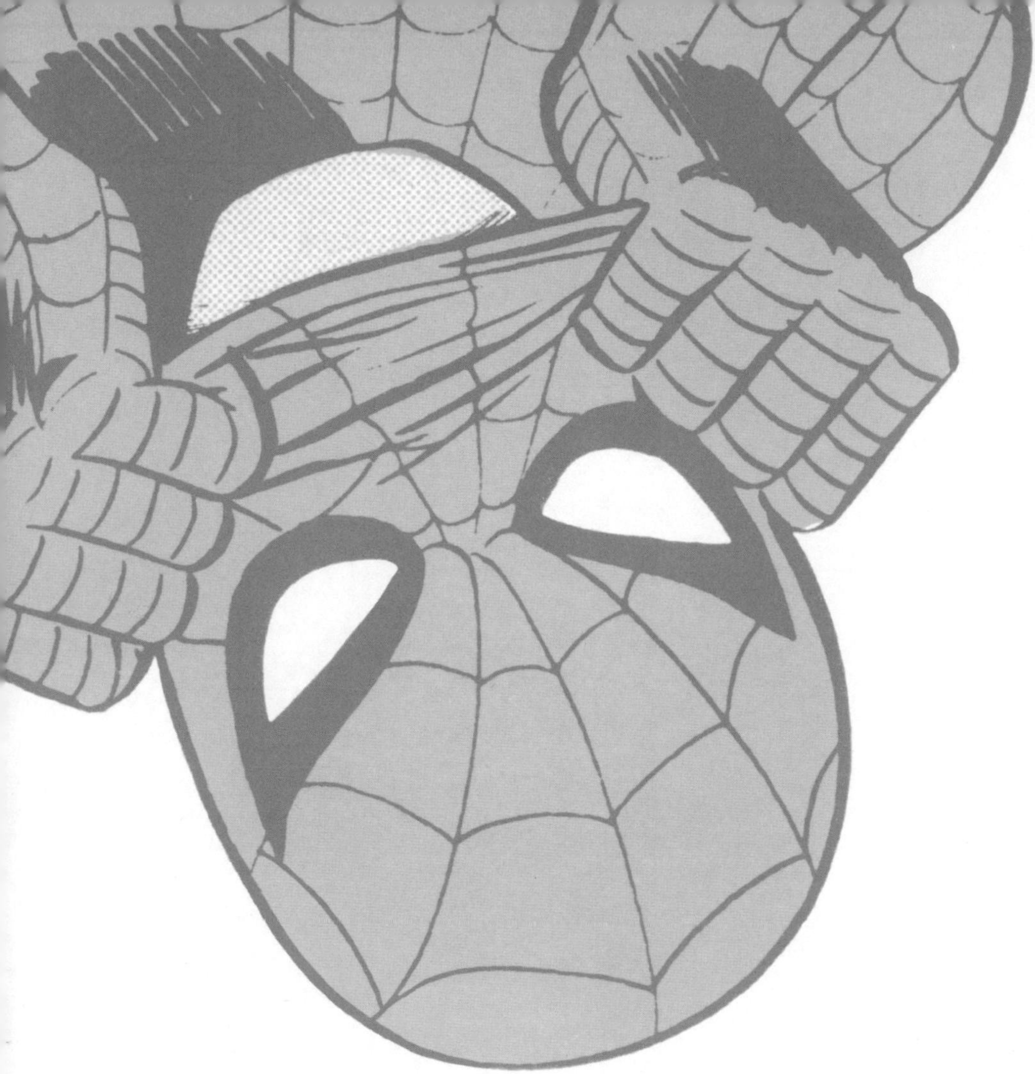

# Introduction

● ● ● ● ● ● ● ● ● ●

In 1965, I received eight well-read comic books as Christmas presents, and I was hooked. During the next several years, I followed the exploits of Spider-Man, Daredevil, and Thor, to the point where I recited dialogue from their stories as my friends and I wrestled. I became so involved with the comic book mythos that I wrote a high-school term paper called, "Comic Books as Literature," and taught a high-school-level course on the history of American comic books.

By the mid-1970s, the artwork and ingenuity that had made comic books so compelling began to lose its grip, and when I sold my collection to supplement my college education, I wasn't sure I'd ever look back. And I didn't; for ten years I read novels, Greek drama and poetry, and entered the teaching profession. And as a teacher I entered the same comic book specialty shop I'd last set foot in a decade before, this time in search of material that would motivate my students to read. While scanning the racks for good stuff I discovered that the comic-book field had changed; superheroes still dominated the industry, but there were other stories, published as graphic novels. These books had a beginning, middle, and end between two covers and attempted to have the same effect as serious prose novels—in other words, the characters grow, change, and reach a point of resolution. I soon found myself researching the graphic-novel field as much for my own interest as for potential reading matter for my students.

In 1987, I left teaching and entered the library profession. As a graduate student, I wrote papers defending the place of Art Spiegelman's *Maus* in the public library, as well as studies of heroism in the work of Jack Kirby. As a working librarian, I struggled to include comic-book materials in the library's collection, and, as a result, library circulation increased and the library swaggered just a bit from a hip appeal.

In 1995, I returned to teaching. This time the classroom was my house and the student was my son, who was having a hard time learning to read. We tried comics, which made a bridge between words and ideas, and pictures and stories. In the course of one academic year he moved up two grade levels in reading comprehension from reading comic books. Two years after that, he was reading prose novels and graphic novels indiscriminately.

The book you hold in your hands is the second revision of the 1996 book, *100 Graphic Novels for Public Libraries,* which grew into *The 101 Best Graphic Novels* (2001) aimed at librarians and general readers. There are several reasons a new edition is needed at this time; many of the books included in the previous editions have gone out of print, and some of the premier cartoonists have created new powerful works that deserve recognition. The manga craze has brought a whole new generation of readers to graphic novels, and Hollywood movies inspired by comic books have energized interest in the comics form.

While compiling the current bibliography, I have dropped picture books and comic strips collections. These are really cousins of the graphic novel; I felt it was more important to focus on actual graphic novels—books with a beginning, middle, and end—this time around. In addition, I chose to include stories of ongoing characters such as Batman, as well as prominent ongoing manga story lines, collected in bound form. Although these stories may be considered soap operas and don't end, many of these works are important contributions to the comics field, and some of these books chronicle a point of discovery within the life of an ongoing character. Further, genre works such as mystery novels have a place in most "best of" lists.

In compiling the current 101 Best list, I consulted some of the bibliographies that have appeared over the last few years, as well as reading extensively on my own. The current bibliography attempts to represent the range of materials published in the graphic novel format currently in print, while pointing out the best books in print at the time of this publication. When identifying the "best" graphic novels, I have sought out those books that have the same qualities that one looks for in a good prose novel—well-drawn characters, realistic plots and settings within the boundaries of their genre, character development, and story resolution. In addition, the artwork propelling the story has to be expressive and telling. I'm also delighted that in this edition includes the Foreword to the original 1996 Kitchen Sink Press book, *100 Graphic Novels for Public Libraries,* written by Neil Gaiman, who was then known primarily as the architect and writer of the *Sandman* graphic novel series, but is now recognized as a world-class prose novelist as well (*American Gods, Coraline*). For this edition, over half the books listed are new. The section of books about comics has been expanded as well because much has been published on graphic novels and comics history during the last few years. Of course every bibliography is limited to the opinions and biases of the person creating it.

Steve Weiner
Maynard, Massachusetts
June 2005

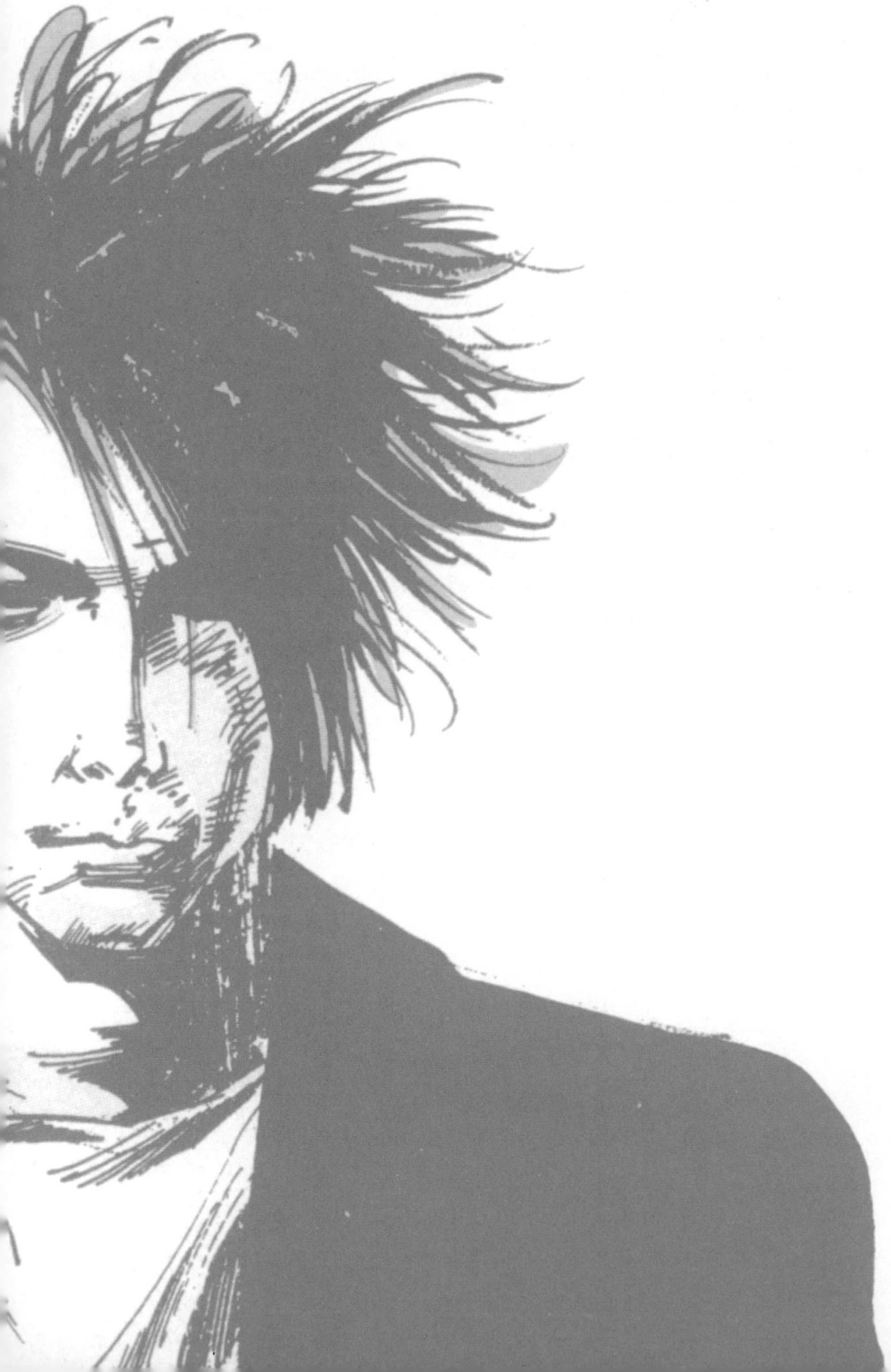

# Foreword

● ● ● ● ● ● ● ●

I grew up in libraries: both the town library, long since demolished, in the English town I lived in as a child, and the libraries of the schools I attended as a boy.

They were the places I went to for recreation and for knowledge.

It was an odd place, the town library, an old building filled with tiny rooms, nooks and crannies, odd corridors that sloped gently downwards. When I was in my teens, they knocked it down, built a new, redbrick, open-plan library with no odd nooks, no strange crannies. I still miss it.

I read there indiscriminately, cementing a relationship with books that's lasted longer than any other friendship, any other love.

In the school holidays, my parents would drop me off on the way to work. I was meant to take sandwiches with me, but sometimes I would forget them. It hardly mattered, though. Hunger for sandwiches was forgotten in the urge to read, to find new ideas, new stories, new ways of telling old stories.

When I finished reading the children's library, I started on the adult library. I started with A.

Let us admit it: I was a boy who loved books. And the library was filled with odd treasures—rare, strange, and delightful books that had, for some reason, caught the librarian's fancy.

No graphic novels, though. This was, after all, quite some time ago.

One problem, reported by many publishers in the U.K. in the early 1990s, as they started publishing graphic novels, was that bookstores were having problems with them—they were getting shoplifted, in quantity. It wasn't that there was no demand for the books: there was an enormous demand. But the readers of the books couldn't always afford them.

On the other hand, at the same time the English libraries that had begun to stock graphic novels had noticed that the books were being checked out, and checked out, and checked out…the readers wanted them, and the graphic novels began to bring new readers into the libraries. Hammersmith Library, in West London, created a specialized graphic novel section, and opened it with a discussion evening that brought people in in record numbers.

Graphic novels brought people into libraries. They made people read.

Comics is a unique medium—a medium as powerful as prose, as drama, as poetry, as film. With, like the other media, its own strengths, its own weaknesses.

Librarians know: every book, every story, is a doorway into another world. Here are a hundred such doorways. May they bring you many readers.

Neil Gaiman
From *100 Graphic Novels for Public Libraries*
1996

# A Brief History of Comics and Graphic Novels

Historians might argue that the first comics were cave paintings depicting battles and tribal rituals, but American comics really began in 1895, with the publication of Richard Outcault's newspaper strip, *The Yellow Kid.* Comic strips caught on, and, as a result, the comic strip became very popular in the early part of the last century. Sunday and daily comic strips continue to be featured in almost every newspaper in the United States.

Comic books were first created in 1933, when Max Gaines bound some newspaper strip reprints together and sold them as a magazine. Soon publishers wanted more than reprinted stories and new material was created for this blossoming form of publishing. For many people who observe the field peripherally, the late 1930s remains a defining moment in both comic book history and popular culture; many of the superheroes who remain popular today were created in the years just prior to World War II.

As a genre, comic books mirrored popular culture. The books published in the 1940s had a distinctly patriotic flavor—indeed many were straight-out Allied propaganda. Comics in the 1950s presented both a conservative viewpoint, found in the popular romance comics, and a growing subversive attitude, as demonstrated in the horror, crime, and science fiction comics published by EC Comics. The 1950s were also the period when the comic book field came under attack as deleterious to the morals of American youth. Dr. Frederic Wertham's book *The Seduction of the Innocent* blamed juvenile delinquency on the effect of comic books. Worried, comic-book publishers created the Comics Code Authority (CCA), which set forth guidelines for acceptable and unacceptable content. EC Comics dropped its controversial comics rather than adopt the CCA's rules, and turned its most successful magazine, *Mad,* into a newsstand periodical not bound by the new regulations. Romances and Western tales flourished.

Superhero comics returned in the late 1950s, and grew very popular in the 1960s. As America had become a more introspective society, the new superheroes, embodied by Spider-Man, were imbued with phobias and challenges. The 1960s also witnessed the emergence of Underground Comix, which, echoing the hippie revolution, expressed discontent with middle class values. Humor, superhero, and other mainstream comic books were sold in drugstores and on newsstands. Underground comix couldn't be sold there because these comics purposefully opposed the mores supported by the CCA. Instead, the undergrounds were sold where their intended audience shopped—head shops. This was the first time anyone had to niche market; previously comic book publishers had attempted to sell to the largest audience possible, but the success of the underground comix movement proved that a profit could be made by appealing directly to readers whose political ideal or artistic aesthetic as the comics creators.

In the late 1970s, the comic book specialty shop appeared. The store was an outgrowth of the comic book conventions of the 1960s, and allowed comic book retailers direct access to comic book collectors and readers. The comic book store supported mainstream comic books as well as undergrounds, perhaps because both forms existed on the fringes of society. The comic-book specialty shop thrived in part because it allowed publishers direct contact with their readership. As a result, many publishers experimented with different kinds of books, each directed at a different segment of the comic store patronage. The store gave birth to a new genre of comic-book publishers: alternative. Some alternative presses published work that might have been supported by mainstream publishers, but instead were brought out by small, startup publishing houses, often allowing the comic-book creator to keep more of the profits.

Other factors were important as well. Cartoonists in the United States were utilizing methods developed by Japanese and European creators, bringing a new sophistication to American comic books. Underground comix moved closer to mainstream comics, virtually disappearing, while some heroes of mainstream books expressed radical political philosophies. The graphic novel, a literary comic book form with a beginning, middle, and end, was popularized by Will Eisner's 1978 book, *A Contract with God and Other Tenement Stories,* four stories about the disenfranchised set in the Bronx during the Great Depression. The book was sold in bookstores rather than comic stores and aimed at adults.

The 1980s brought forth a new, tortured superhero. These stories were not meant for ten-year-old boys, but to ten-year-olds who had matured but still wanted to read comic books. Artwork became more expressive and storylines increasingly demanding. Comic readers had to grow more literary to comprehend the involved storylines. Ironically, comic books, and their grown-up counterpart, graphic novels, became more literate at the same time that national reading scores began to decline.

Toward the end of the 1980s and into the 1990s, the graphic-novel form grew in popularity. The form had many advantages; because it told a complete story, it became an easy way for readers unfamiliar with comic books to try these books, and regular comic-book readers who had grown tired of missing an issue in the middle of an ongoing storyline could now read the piece as a whole. By the late 1990s, public libraries were adding graphic novels to their popular collections, and graphic novels were being awarded prizes previously given only to prose works.

In the early part of the twenty-first century, bookstores began adding graphic novels to their vast array of reading choices, as comics made further inroads into popular culture thanks to a string of highly successful motion pictures based on comic-book characters, serious novels set in the world of comic books, graphic novels presenting serious subjects with sensitivity, and the explosion of interest in manga that was emigrating to the United States from Japan. Since 2002, the graphic-novel form has grown so popular that not only do most major bookstores have a graphic novel section, most trade publishing houses now have some kind of graphic novel publishing program. This, combined with the traditional avenues for comic-book publishing, has made the graphic novel a more visible and viable form than it's ever been in American culture, as readers are given a wider array of types of stories told in comic book form than ever before.

And who knows what the future will bring?

# Author's Acknowledgements

For their help with this book,
the author would like to thank:

Chris Couch
Tony Davis
Lee Dawson
Keith R.A. DeCandido
The late Will Eisner
Neil Gaiman
Craig Shaw Gardner
Chris Golden
Judy Hansen
The librarians at the Maynard Public Library in Massachusetts
The members of the online discussion group GNLIB-L
David Hyde
Rachel Korn
Denis Kitchen
Michael Martins
Scott McCloud
Mike Mignola
Terry Nantier
Eric Reynolds
Chris Shadoian
Bill Sleator
Jeff Smith
Chris Staros
Julian Weiner
Lily Weiner

And of course, those people whose
names I forgot to list here.

# THE 101 BEST GRAPHIC NOVELS

Each book is
assigned a readership level:

**C**  Books for readers of all ages,
    especially readers 12 and under.

**Y**  For readers between 12 and 15.

**Y+** For teens between 16 and 19.

**A**  For readers 20 years old
    and older.

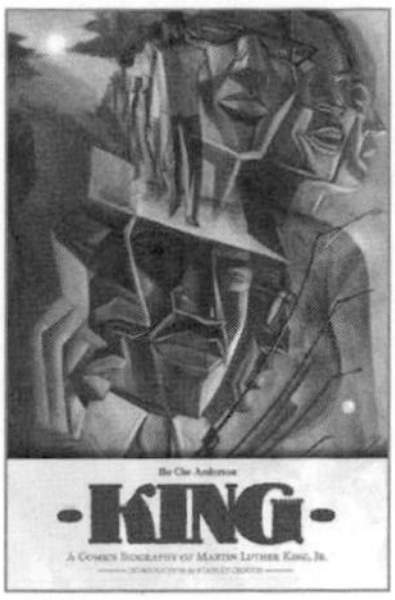
-KING-

**Anderson, Ho Che**
***King: A Comics Biography of Martin Luther King, Jr.***
**Fantagraphics Books, 2005**
**ISBN 1560976225**
**$22.95**
**Y+**

Anderson's compassionate, insightful biography of Martin Luther King was ten years in the making and is at once humanizing and historically accurate, and follows the civil rights leader from his early days to the marches on Washington to the final days in April 1968, when he was assassinated at the age of thirty-nine. Anderson's style is mesmerizing, mixing cinematic and cartooning techniques, and moves easily from black and white to color and back again.

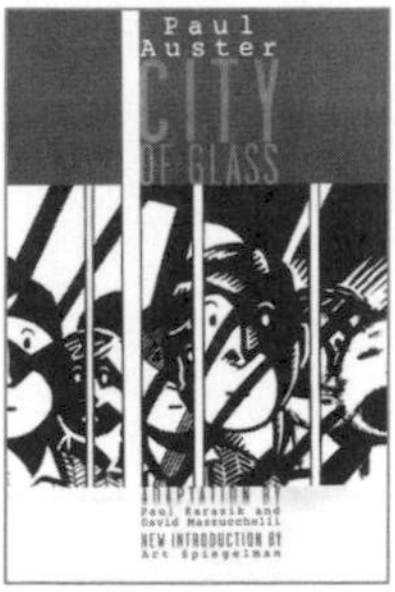
Paul
Auster
CITY
OF GLASS

**Auster, Paul**
**(adapted by Paul Karasik and David Mazzucchelli)**
***City of Glass***
**Picador, 2004**
**ISBN 0312423608**
**$14.00**
**Y+**

Presented almost as a mystery prose novel and told in dramatic black-and-white illustrations that expand upon Auster's original premise, this book becomes a not only a mystery story, but a commentary about the mystery novel format itself.

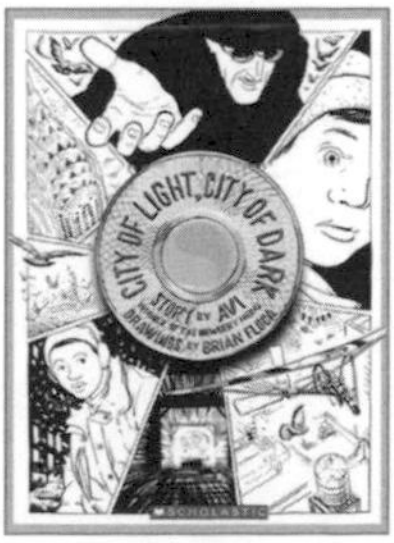
CITY OF LIGHT, CITY OF DARK

**Avi & Brian Floca**
***City of Light, City of Dark: A Comic Book Novel***
**Scholastic, 2004**
**ISBN 0531070581**
**$8.99**
**C**

In this short novel, heroine Estella defeats the Kurds by finding a key and thus saving the city. The illustrations are reminiscent of the work of Louis Slobodkin, and nicely complement the text by Newbery Award-winner Avi.

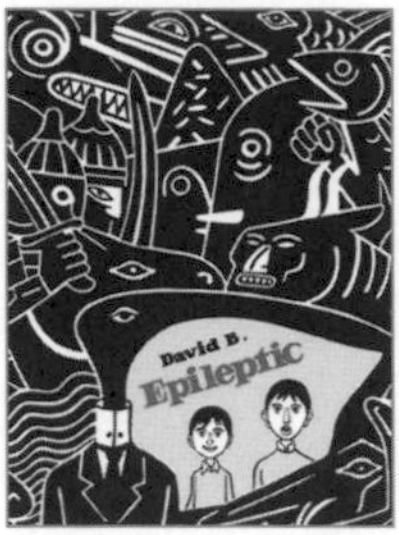
David B.
Epileptic

**B., David**
***Epileptic***
**Pantheon Books, 2005**
**ISBN 0375423184**
**$25.00**
**Y+**

In this deeply affecting memoir which has been compared to James Joyce's novel, *A Portrait of the Artist as a Young Man,* French cartoonist David B. describes his parents relentless attempts to find a remedy for his brother's epilepsy, as the family tries Western medicine, macrobiotic diets, and magnetic and other alternative therapies, all the while journeying deeply into alternative lifestyles and trying to ward off debilitating depression. There are three things that make this graphic novel brilliant: the depiction of epilepsy, the artist's style, which moves from the cartoony to the terrifying effortlessly and without notice, and David B.'s unflinching honesty, as he depicts his own life in many ways as a response to his brother's progressing illness.

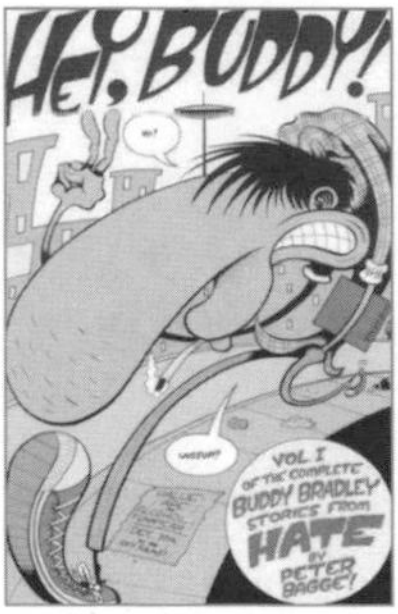
HEY, BUDDY!
VOL. I OF THE COMPLETE BUDDY BRADLEY STORIES FROM HATE BY PETER BAGGE

**Bagge, Peter**
***Hey Buddy!: Volume 1 of the Complete Buddy Bradley Stories from Hate***
**Fantagraphics Books, 1997**
**ISBN 1560971134**
**$12.95**
**A**

*Hate* is Peter Bagge's ode to those who live on the edge, whose world consists of comic book shops, used record- and bookstores, and whose idea of horror is holding a job requiring some responsibility. *Hey Buddy!* is an engaging look at peripheral people who exist primarily for the next issue, next CD, or next book sale. One can sense the influence of Robert Crumb in these black-and-white illustrations.

**Baker, Kyle**
*Why I Hate Saturn*
DC Comics, 1998
ISBN 0930289722
$17.95
Y

Annie and Ricky are fringe players, who eke out a living as columnists for *Daddy-O,* a magazine appealing to the the hip and disenfranchised. When Annie's crazy sister suddenly reappears, Annie is forced to make a commitment to someone other than herself. In doing so, she willingly puts herself in danger and confronts the U.S. military. *Why I Hate Saturn* is saturated with irreverence and tongue-in-cheek humor.

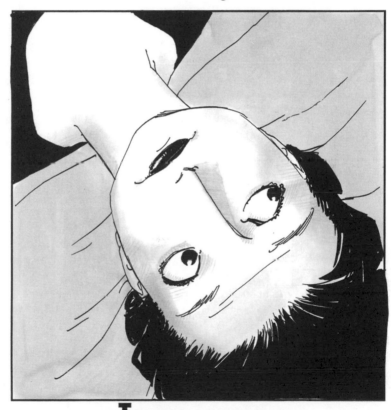

That night, I had a horrible nightmare.
I dreamed that Laura had broken into the apartment while I was out,
and she had written 'Wash me' in the dust all over my apartment.

I was awakened by the doorbell.

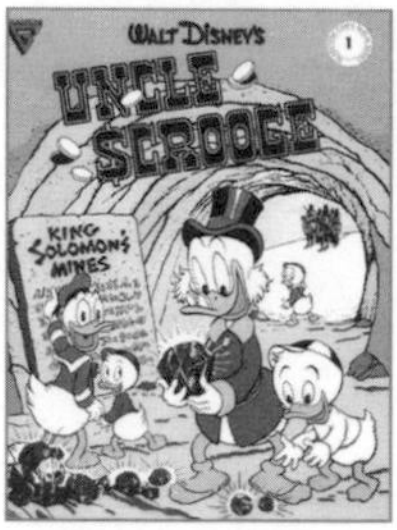
Walt Disney's
Uncle Scrooge
King Solomon's Mines

**Barks, Carl**
***Walt Disney's Uncle Scrooge: The Mines of King Solomon***
**Gladstone Publishing, 1987**
**ISBN 0944599001**
**$5.95**
**C**

Barks, one of the great illustrators in American comics history, was also writing excellent children's fiction. In this adventure, Uncle Scrooge, Donald, Huey, Louie and Dewey go to sixty-nine countries and cross all seven seas.

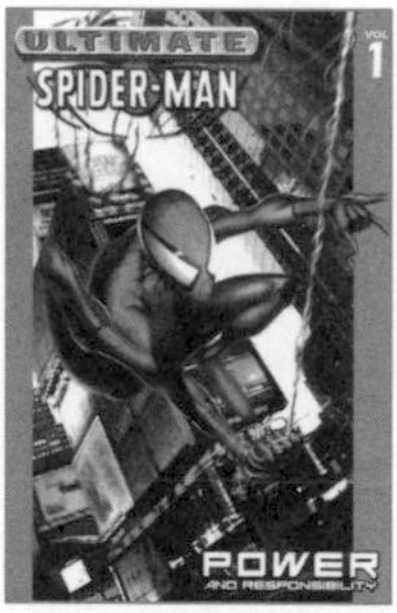
Ultimate
Spider-Man
1
Power

**Bendis, Brian Michael & Mark Bagley**
***The Ultimate Spider-Man: Power and Responsibility***
**Marvel Entertainment Group, 2001**
**ISBN 078510786X**
**$14.95**
**Y**

This reworking of Spider-Man's origin has been updated for today's readers by including modern references and splashy artwork. In a form true to the original Spider-Man from the 1960s, Spider-Man's personal problems are harder to resolve than his fights with super-villains. More stories of Spider-Man are collected in succeeding *Ultimate Spider-Man* books. Also recommended: *The Ultimate X-Men* also by Bendis and others.

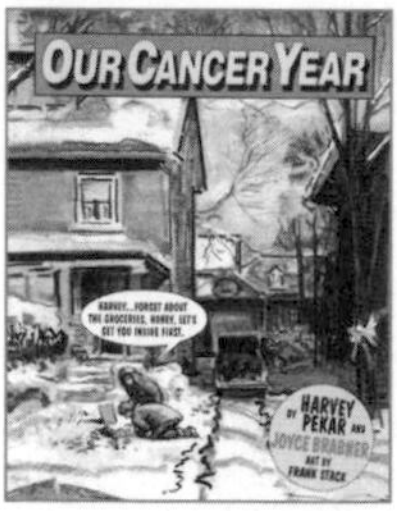
Our Cancer Year
Harvey Pekar

**Brabner, Joyce, Harvey Pekar & Frank Stack**
***Our Cancer Year***
**Four Walls, Eight Windows, 1994**
**ISBN 1568580118**
**$17.95**
**A**

This account of Pekar's battle with cancer as told by him and his coauthor/wife Brabner is illustrated with compassion by Frank Stack. The result is a gut-wrenching reading experience.

CLUMSY
A NOVEL
BY JEFFREY BROWN

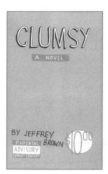

**Brown, Jeffrey**
***Clumsy***
**Top Shelf Productions, 2003**
**ISBN 0971359768**
**$10.00**
**A**

Presented as autobiography, this book chronicles the new relationship between art student Jeffrey and Theresa, a potter. Told episodically, and with poetic simplicity, in small black and white pictures, this book is a standout because it conveys the small ways relationships grow and change.

I NEVER LIKED YOU
CHESTER BROWN

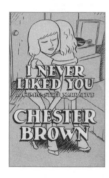

**Brown, Chester**
***I Never Liked You***
**Drawn & Quarterly, 1994**
**ISBN 0969670168**
**$12.95**
**A**

Brown's biting commentary on adolescent insecurity and search for love is moving and true to life. The book design is particularly effective in conveying teen isolation and yearning. This is one of the best graphic novels articulating a realistic coming of age. For readers who read (and re-read) J.D. Salinger's *The Catcher in the Rye.*

I NEVER LIKED YOU YOU KNOW! I NEVER LIKED YOU!
I KNOW.

Kurt Busiek's
Astro City
Life in the Big City

**Busiek, Kurt & Brent Anderson**
***Kurt Busiek's Astro City: Life in the Big City***
**DC Comics, 1999**
**ISBN 156389551X**
**$19.95**
**Y**

This tribute to golden age superhero lore is a charmer. Busiek plays both raconteur and historian in this collection from the serial, as he aptly tells a variety of tales about the heroes of Astro City, from Samaritan, who quests for a normal life, but is prevented from it by world saving and crime fighting, to a thug who accidentally discovers Jack-in-the-Box's secret identity, a revelation that does not bring him the good fortune he expects. Anderson's illustrations are slow and musing, providing a good vehicle for these stories. Other titles include *Family Album, Confessions,* and *The Tarnished Angel.*

JESUS!
I MAKE A NOTE TO TRY NOT TO WASTE TIME LIKE THAT IN THE FUTURE --
-- AND I HOLD THE BUILDING TOGETHER WHILE THEY EVACUATE IT.

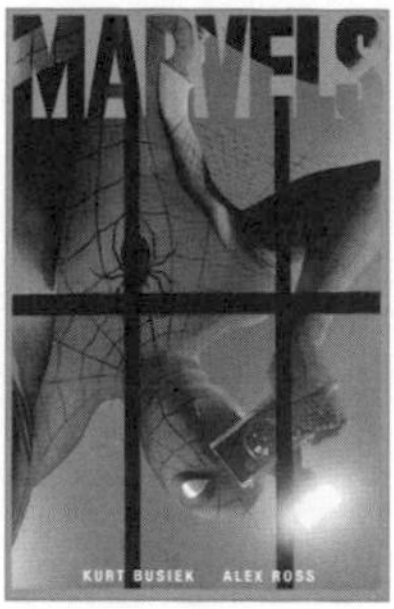
MARVELS
KURT BUSIEK ALEX ROSS

**Busiek, Kurt & Alex Ross**
***Marvels***
**Marvel Entertainment Group, 2004**
**ISBN 0785113886**
**$49.99**
**Y**

Throughout the history of superhero comics, the newspaper profession has played a pivotal role. The secret identities of both Superman and Spider-Man are journalists. The protagonist of *Marvels* is a photographer who has no other identity, but tries to document how normal people feel as they walk among the super-powered. *Marvels* probably resonates more strongly with readers familiar with the Marvel superhero universe, but is still a very compelling look at the normal-person's view of a super-world.

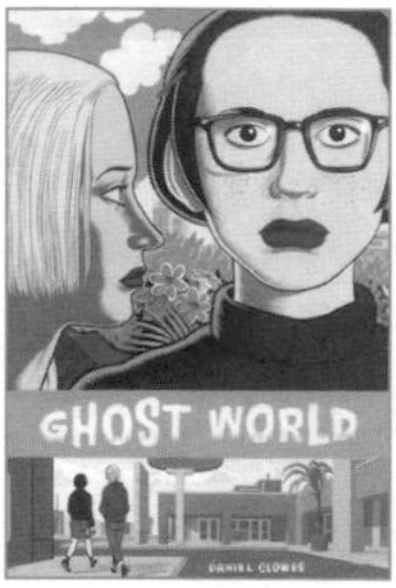
GHOST WORLD

**Clowes, Daniel**
***Ghost World***
**Fantagraphics Books, 2001**
**ISBN 1560974273**
**$11.95**
**A**

Enid and Becky are codependent friends as high school ends. However, Enid's vague desire to attend college drives them apart, and Becky develops a relationship with Josh, whom Enid also admires. Becky's relationship with Josh helps distance her from Enid. Enid's efforts to overcome her jealousy and her decision at the book's resolution is shattering and surprising, as true revelations are in all fiction, and readers are left to ponder how life decisions are made. Beautifully illustrated. (Also the basis of a 2000 feature film.)

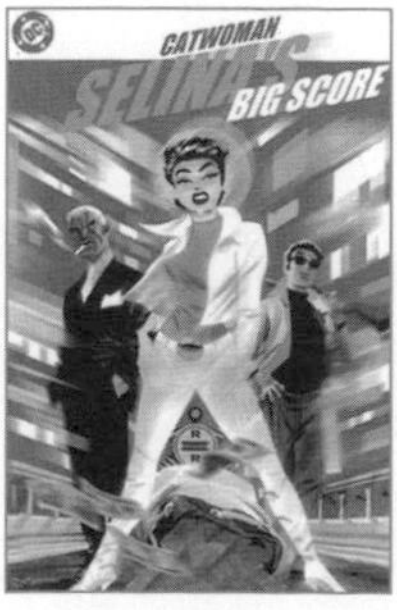
CATWOMAN
BIG SCORE

**Cooke, Darwyn**
***Catwoman: Selina's Big Score***
**DC Comics, 2003**
**ISBN 1563899221**
**$17.95**
**Y**

This incarnation of the Catwoman saga opens with Catwoman

accused of murdering her other identity, Selina Kyle. After laying low, Selina takes up with Chantel and the two plan to steal twenty-four million dollars and hope to use it to help family members in need. To accomplish this, Selina bring in her old mentor/lover Stark. Detective Slam Bradley is out looking for Catwoman. Things go awry; at the story's end Chantel and Stark are dead, and Slam Bradley has a bullet wound. Cooke artfully melds themes made popular in the Frank Miller Daredevil and Batman graphic novels with cinematic cartooning. Be careful what you wish for.

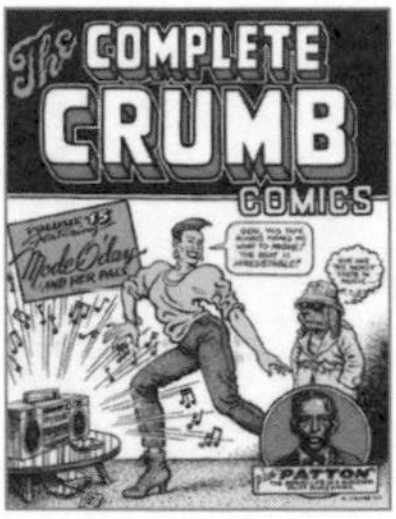
The COMPLETE
CRUMB
COMICS

**Crumb, R**
***The Complete Crumb Comics Volume 15 Featuring Modele Oday and Her Pals***
**Fantagraphics Books, 2002**
**ISBN 1560974133**
**$18.95**
**Y+**

One of the most influential and original cartoonists in the history of American comics, and the subject of a mainstream film, Robert Crumb's work is recognized as a driving force in popular culture. This volume in the *Complete Crumb* series introduces the Modele Oday strip and includes collaborations with Charles Bukowski and Harvey Pekar. Fantagraphics Books has collected the entire Crumb oeuvre in seventeen volumes.

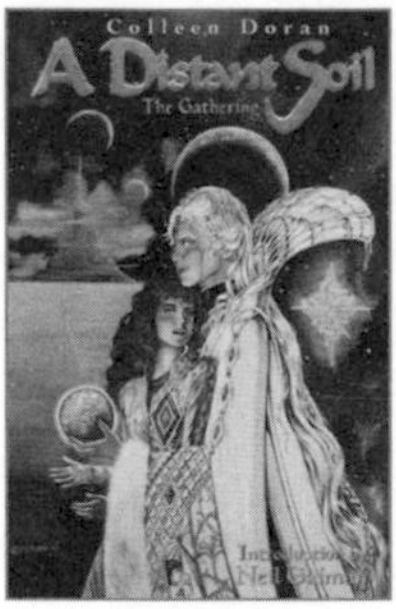
Colleen Doran
A Distant Soil
The Gathering

**Doran, Colleen**
***A Distant Soil: The Gathering***
**Image Comics, 2001**
**ISBN 1887279512**
**$19.95**
**Y**

When Liana and Jason accidentally kill a guard while escaping from the research institution where they've been living they don't realize that their problems are just beginning. Inheriting her alien father's extraordinary psychic powers, Liana is one of the most powerful forces in the universe, putting Liana and Jason in the middle of a universal power struggle. Other volumes in the series include *Knights of the Angel, The Ascendant, The Aria,* and *Coda.*

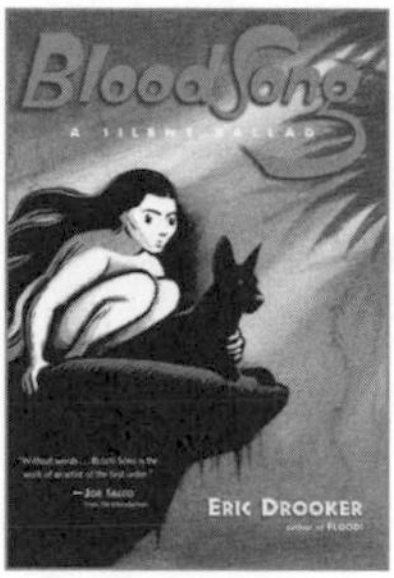
Blood Song
A SILENT BALLAD
ERIC DROOKER

**Drooker, Eric**
***Blood Song: A Silent Ballad***
**Harvest Books, 2002**
**ISBN 015600884X**
**$20.00**
**Y+**

When the military invade a young woman's fishing village, she and her dog escape by rowing across the ocean. Arriving in a city, she becomes involved with a street musician whom the authorities arrest because his songs are a disturbance. While the musician is imprisoned the young woman bears a child, who is born singing. *Blood Song* is a wordless graphic novel illustrated by a series of interconnected scratchboard drawings. Also recommended is Drooker's earlier book, *Flood!* about urban life on the verge of collapse.

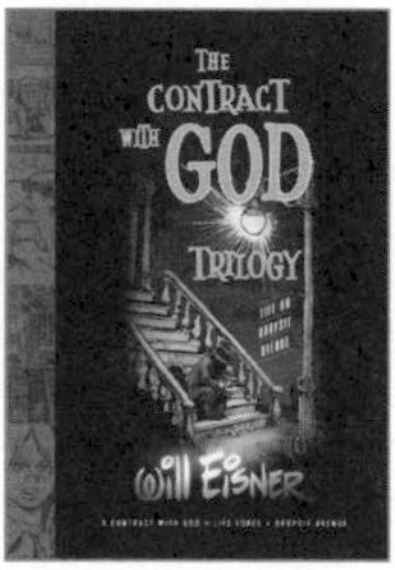
THE CONTRACT WITH GOD TRILOGY
WILL EISNER

**Eisner, Will**
***A Contract with God Trilogy***
**W.W. Norton, 2005**
**ISBN 0393061051**
**$29.95**
**Y+**

This book collects three of Eisner's books, all depicting life on the imaginary Dropsie Avenue in the Bronx: *A Contract with God and Other Tenement Stories, A Life Force,* and *Dropsie Avenue: the Neighborhood. Contract,* which consists of four thematically linked stories, focuses on the story of Frimme Hersh, a good man, who feels that God has betrayed him. First published in 1978, *Contract* is also recognized by many as the first modern graphic novel. *A Life Force,* one of Eisner's most realized works, tells the story of Jacob Shtarkah, a carpenter with a weak heart and a poetic bent, intent on living a meaningful life. *Dropsie Avenue* chronicles the changing life on Dropsie Avenue from the arrival of Dutch immigrants in the 1600s, and follows waves of immigration and the changing political climate through American history, in the microcosm of one city block.

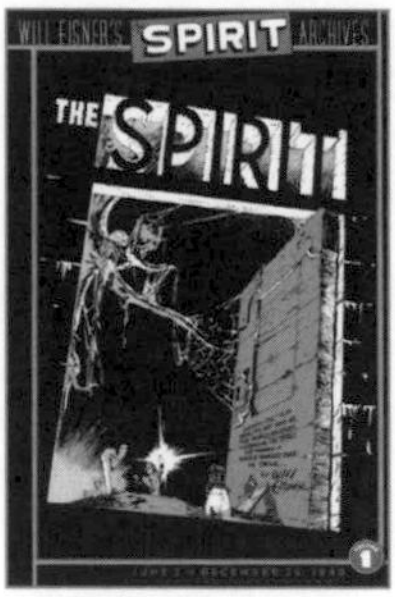
WILL EISNER'S SPIRIT ARCHIVES
THE SPIRIT

**Eisner, Will**
***The Spirit Archives, Volume 1***
**DC Comics, 2000**
**ISBN 1563896737**
**$49.95**
**C**

This reprints the first six months of the immensely popular and influential strip by Eisner. Lawman Denny Colt put on a mask and called himself the Spirit in order to fight crime. Although a simple adventure comic on the face of it, *The Spirit* revolutionized sequential art storytelling.

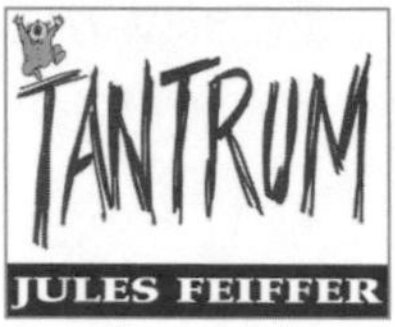
TANTRUM
JULES FEIFFER

**Feiffer, Jules**
***Tantrum!***
**Fantagraphics Books, 1997**
**ISBN 1560972823**
**$16.95**
**A**

This drama of midlife crisis is as compelling today as when it first appeared. Protagonist Leo asks: What is the value of growing older? As a reaction to middle age, Leo reverts to babyhood. However, with the wisdom of years, can childhood remain innocent? The "splash and scratch" drawings move the narrative forward with almost mindless speed.

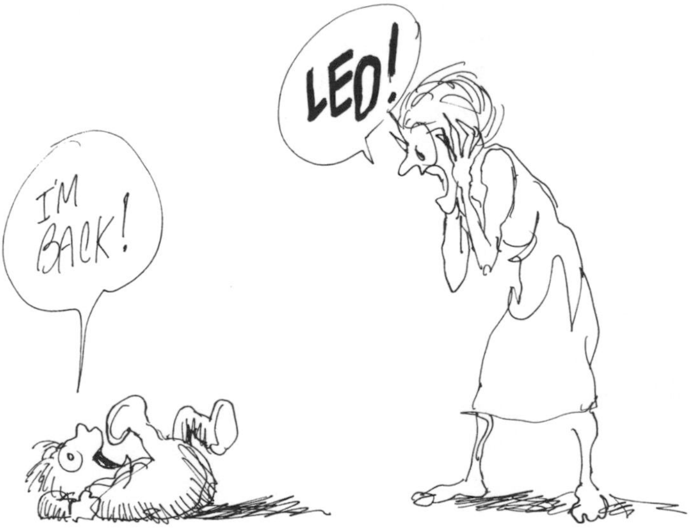
LEO!
I'M BACK!

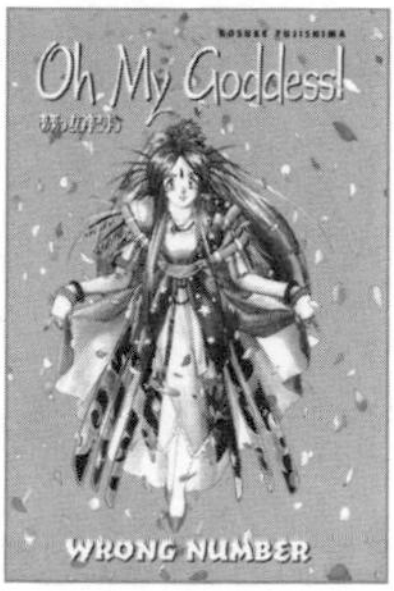
Oh My Goddess!
WRONG NUMBER

**Fujishima, Kosuke**
***Oh My Goddess: Wrong Number***
**Dark Horse, 2002**
**ISBN 1569716692**
**$13.95**
**Y**

When college student Keichi Morisato dials the Goddess Technical Help Line, a goddess appears in his dorm room, eager to grant him one wish. Impulsively, Keichi wishes that the goddess stay with him always. This new arrangement, once granted, presents problems, as the goddess has been stripped of most of her power and doesn't understand Keichi's world, causing as much trouble as she solves. By turns humorous, adventure-filled, and touched with romance, this book is a pleasure. This is an ongoing series.

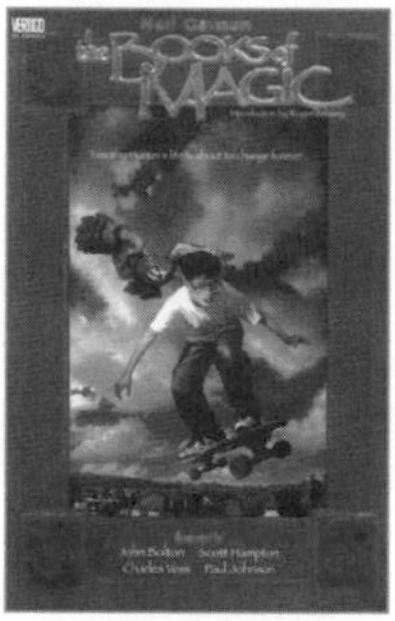
the BOOKS of MAGIC

**Gaiman, Neil, et al**
***The Books of Magic***
**DC Comics, 1993**
**ISBN 1563890828**
**$19.95**
**Y**

In a story reminiscent of the British fantasists Alan Garner and Susan Cooper, young Tim Hunter reluctantly joins a magic circle that he will someday rule. Arthurian fantasy doesn't translate into the graphic novel medium better than this.

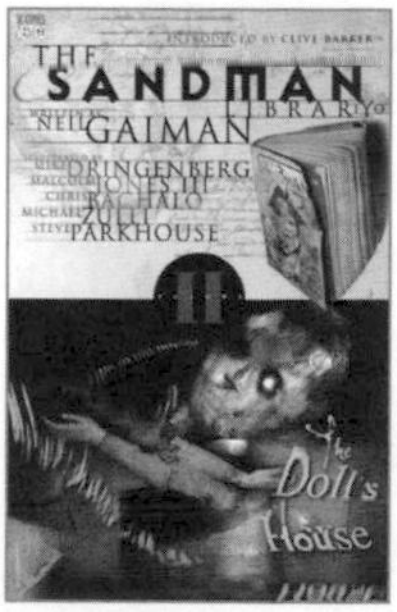
THE SANDMAN
NEIL GAIMAN
The Doll's House

**Gaiman, Neil, et al**
***The Sandman: The Doll's House***
**DC Comics, 1999**
**ISBN 1563892251**
**$19.99**
**A**

Gaiman's *The Sandman* monthly series was a reinvention of a minor 1940s hero, and Gaiman drew extensively on world mythologies, binding storylines of fragile humans and deities older than gods to create a seamless tapestry upon which compelling stories are told. *Sandman* was mainstream comics' most serious attempt to create a new mythology for adults, and this particular story, *The Doll's House,* articulates Gaiman's answer as to why gods exist. Other titles include *Brief Lives, Dream Country, The Dream Hunters, Endless Nights, Fables and Reflections, A Game of You, The Kindly Ones, King of Dreams, Preludes and Nocturnes, The Quotable Sandman, The Sandman Companion, Season of Mists, The Wake,* and *World's End.*

MR. PUNCH

**Gaiman, Neil & Dave McKean**
***Mr. Punch***
**DC Comics, 1995**
**ISBN 1563892464**
**$19.95**
**Y**

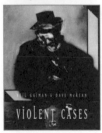

VIOLENT CASES

**Gaiman, Neil & Dave McKean**
***Violent Cases***
**Dark Horse, 2003**
**ISBN 1569716064**
**$14.95**
**Y**

Writer Gaiman and artist McKean team for these two very different tales. *Mr. Punch* is a chilly contemporary version of the medieval "Punch and Judy" play, which is painted in watercolor, and steeped in mythology, folklore, and literature. *Violent Cases* begins as a mystery/gangster story, but it evolves into a study of memory and desire, and readers are chilled by the ironic conclusion. McKean's art is sure and narrative, and the characters are distinct while remaining distant. Take your hat off while you read this one.

I went and hid in some bushes, and waited.
After five minutes,-
the car came cruising
slowly
back down the road.
It went past three times, before I came out of the woods

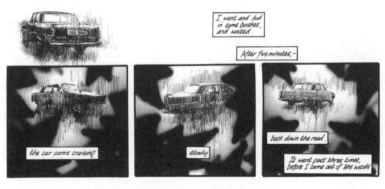

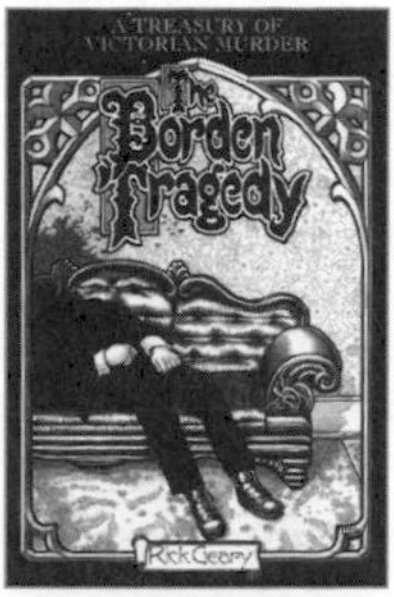
A TREASURY OF
VICTORIAN MURDER
The Borden Tragedy
Rick Geary

**Geary, Rick**
***The Borden Tragedy: A Memoir of the Infamous Double Murder at Fall River, Mass., 1892***
**NBM, 1997**
**ISBN 1561631892**
**$8.95**
**Y**

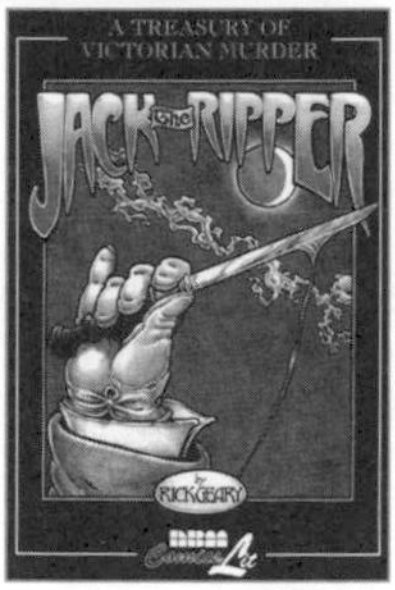
A TREASURY OF
VICTORIAN MURDER
JACK the RIPPER
RICK GEARY

**Geary, Rick**
***Jack the Ripper: A Journal of the Whitechapel Murders 1888-1889***
**NBM, 2001**
**ISBN 1561633089**
**$7.95**
**Y**

These two little books are part of Geary's "Treasury of Victorian Murder" series. *The Borden Tragedy* presents a restrained account of the infamous double slaying, as told by an anonymous observer close to the Borden family. Readers sympathize with the public smearing of Lisbeth "Lizzie" Borden, and are relieved at the trial's outcome. Geary wryly notes the similarities between the Borden trial of the 1890s and the O.J. Simpson trial of the 1990s. In *Jack the Ripper,* Geary turns an impartial and clear eye on the horrific crimes committed against prostitutes in Whitechapel. The illustrations are poignant, unsentimental, and move the narratives along handily. Both volumes include a bibliography. (See also Alan Moore & Eddie Campbell's *From Hell.*)

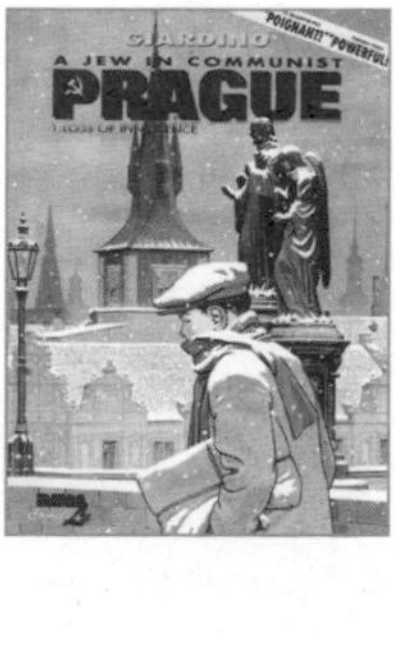
A JEW IN COMMUNIST
PRAGUE

**Giardino, Vittorio**
***A Jew in Communist Prague. Volume 1: Loss of Innocence***
**NBM, 1997**
**ISBN 1561631809**
**$11.95**
**A**

This first book in the series recounts the childhood of Jonas Finkel, whose father is mysteriously taken by the police in 1950 communist Prague. Young Finkel is victimized by anti-Semitism, removed from school, forced to work as an errand boy, and isolated from his peers. The story ends hopefully as

Jonas and his mother learn that his father is alive and held in a prison camp. Told in clear, understated illustrations, and colored primarily with greens and blues, this graphic novel offers a touch of Kafka while being gentle on the eyes. Volumes 2 and 3 are also available: *Adolescence* and *Rebellion.*

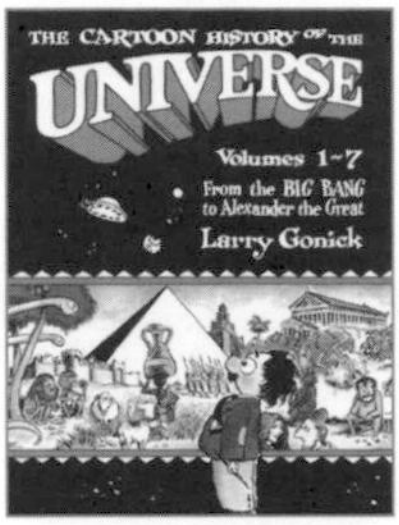
THE CARTOON HISTORY OF THE
UNIVERSE
Volumes 1-7
From the BIG BANG to Alexander the Great
Larry Gonick

**Gonick, Larry**
***Larry Gonick's The Cartoon History of the Universe.***
**William Morrow, 1982**
**ISBN 0688010113**
**$11.00**
**Y**
One of the most popular, widely read and reviewed books in the graphic novel format, this book provides clear historical information using a visual orientation and a humorous approach.

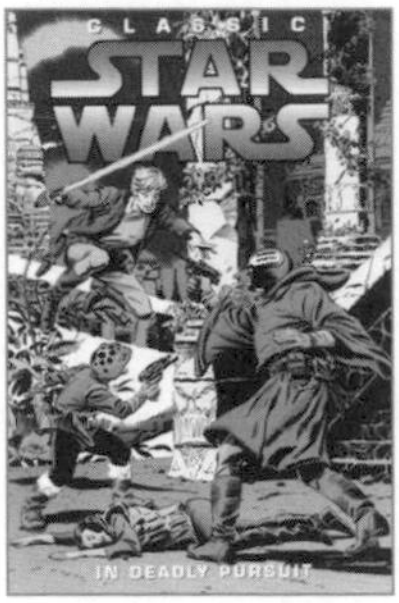
CLASSIC
STAR WARS
IN DEADLY PURSUIT

**Goodwin, Archie & Al Williamson**
***Classic Star Wars***
**Dark Horse, 1995**
**ISBN 1569711097**
**$16.95**
**Y**
Goodwin's facile scripts and Williamson's cinematic art retell and expand on the *Star Wars* movie themes in this collection of the first *Star Wars* newspaper strips published from 1981-1984.

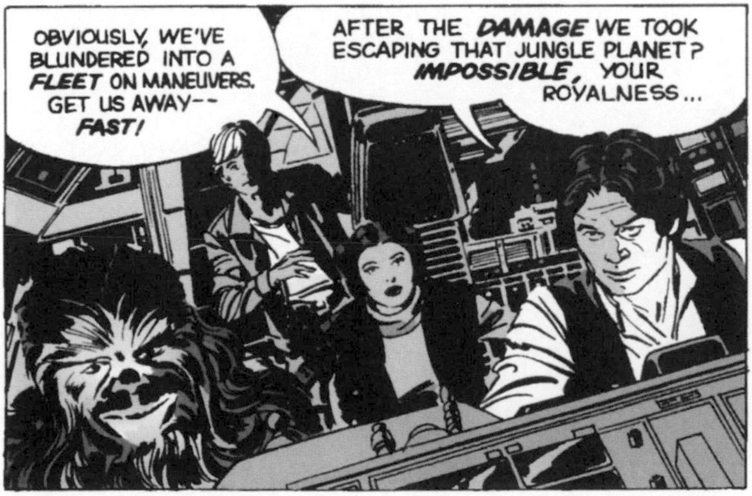
OBVIOUSLY, WE'VE BLUNDERED INTO A FLEET ON MANEUVERS. GET US AWAY-- FAST!
AFTER THE DAMAGE WE TOOK ESCAPING THAT JUNGLE PLANET? IMPOSSIBLE, YOUR ROYALNESS...

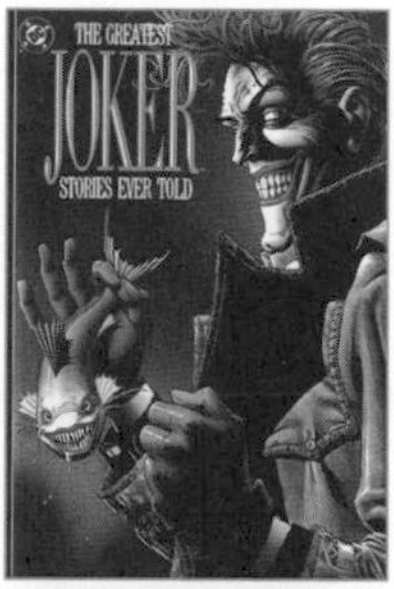
THE GREATEST
JOKER
STORIES EVER TOLD

*The Greatest Joker Stories Ever Told*
**DC Comics, 1997**
**$14.95**
**ISBN 0930289366**
**C**

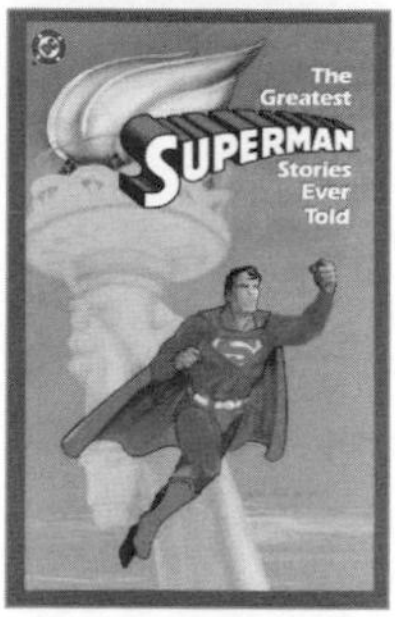
The Greatest
SUPERMAN
Stories Ever Told

*The Greatest Superman Stories Ever Told*
**DC Comics, 1986**
**ISBN 0930289390**
**$15.95**
**C**

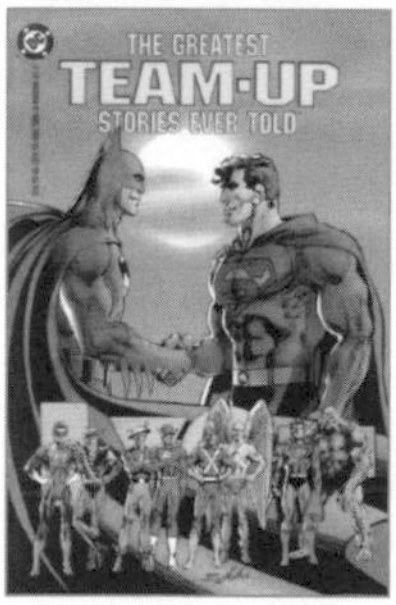
THE GREATEST
TEAM-UP
STORIES EVER TOLD

*The Greatest Team-Up Stories Ever Told*
**DC Comics, 1991**
**ISBN 0930289617**
**$14.95**
**C**

These volumes collect stories from over five decades' of comics history, including various interpretations of Batman's arch-enemy, the Joker; a wide range of Superman stories, from the simplistic to the self-doubting; and some fine examples of heroes working together, the best of which is a surprising Superman/Swamp Thing pairing.

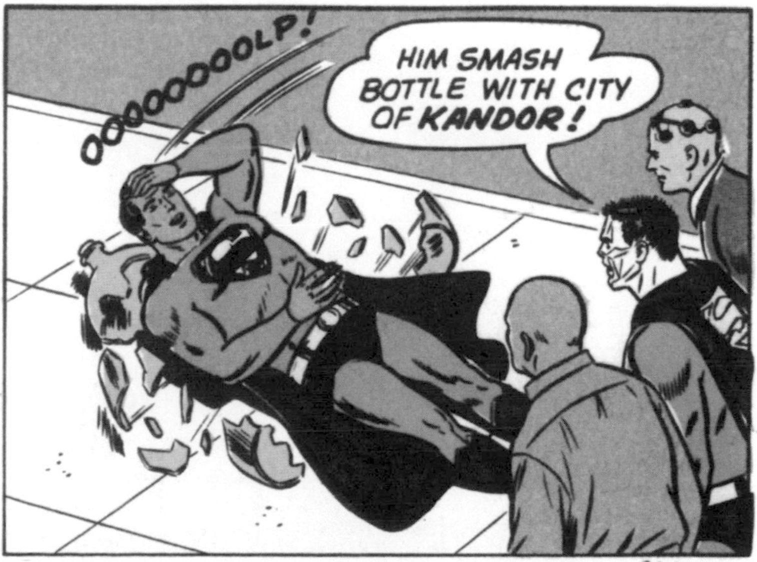
OOOOOOOOOLP!
HIM SMASH BOTTLE WITH CITY OF KANDOR!

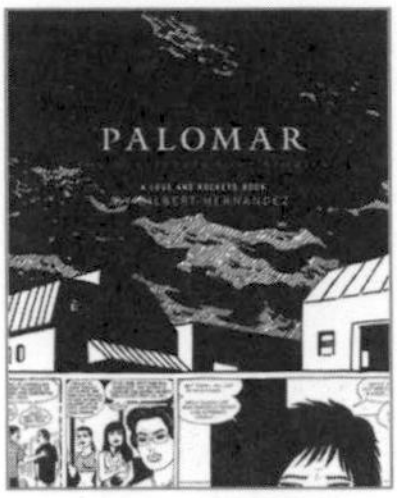
PALOMAR

**Hernandez, Gilbert**
***Palomar: The Heartbreak Soup Stories***
**Fantagraphic Books, 2003**
**ISBN 1560975393**
**$39.95**
**Y+**

A mythical Latin American village, Palomar is a town whose residents live out unexceptional lives. Then Luba arrives, becoming one of the leaders of Palomar. This book chronicles the events in the town from Luba's arrival to her departure twenty years later. Cartoonist Gilbert Hernandez and his brother Jaime co-created *Love & Rockets* in the early 1980s, from which these stories are selected. *Love & Rockets* encompassed a broad ensemble of characters, broke new ground in both the subject matter and the way comics stories were told. The book was identified as one of the secret masterpieces of American fiction by *Rolling Stone* magazine, and appealed to female as well as male readers. Some of Jaime's stories have been collected in the companion volume to *Palomar: Locas: The Maggie and Hopey Stories.*

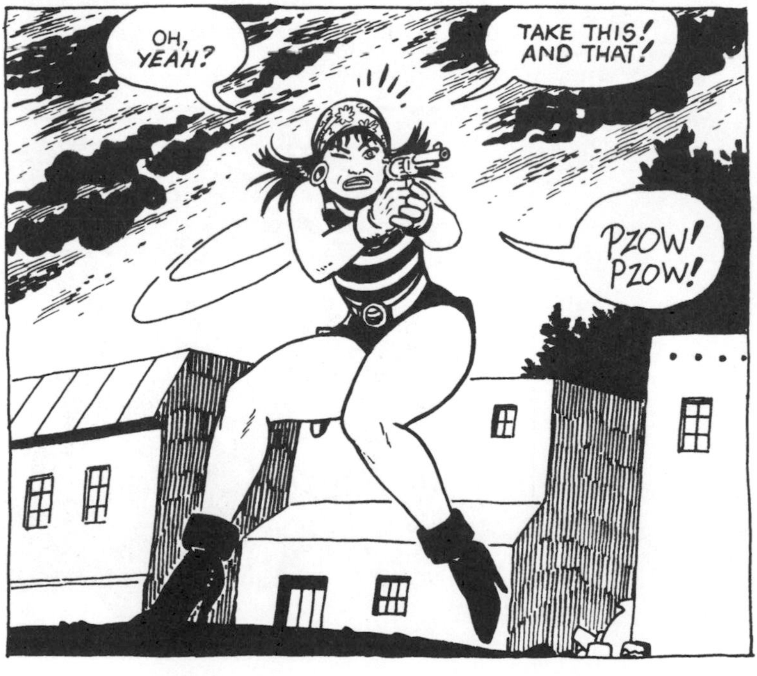
TAKE THIS! AND THAT!
OH, YEAH?
PZOW! PZOW!

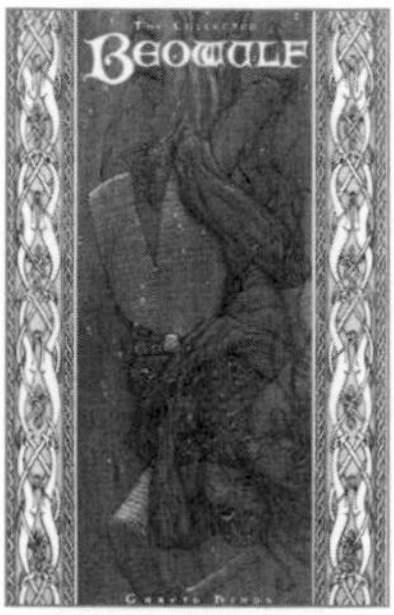
Beowulf

**Hinds, Gareth**
***The Collected Beowulf***
**thecomic.com, 2000**
**ISBN 1893131041**
**$15.95**
**Y**

Based on a 1910 translation, this version of the Beowulf saga feels like an artifact from old England: hard and unforgiving. Using words sparingly, Hinds does not count on readers knowing the story, but instead is intent on retelling it his way, slowly, with emphasis on life in post-Arthurian Europe. An excellent introduction to a classic story. Also recommended by Hinds: *Bearskin: A Grimm Tale.*

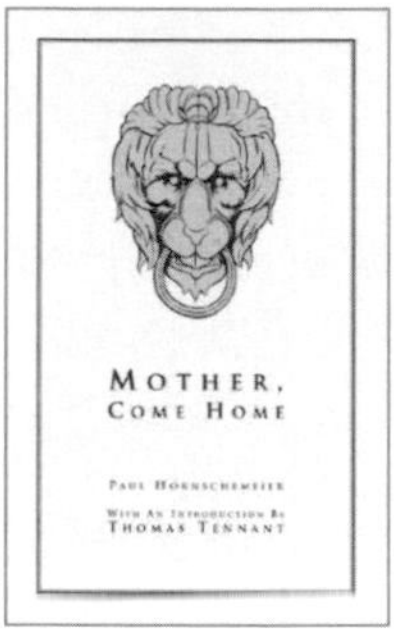
Mother,
Come Home

**Hornschemeier, Paul**
***Mother Come Home***
**Dark Horse, 2003**
**ISBN 1593070373**
**$14.95**
**Y**

*Mother Come Home* tells the story of a father and son's attempts to recover from the death of the family's mother from cancer. Each retreat into a fantasy world of their own—the protagonist into a child's power fantasy while the father suffers a breakdown. Brilliantly illustrated in soft, cartoony drawings, the story's conclusion is genuine, unforced, and shattering. One of the most honest graphic novels ever published.

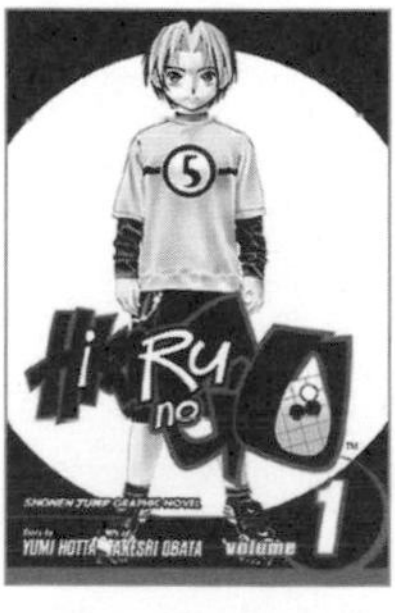

**Hotta, Yumi, with Takehi Obata**
***Hikaru No Go***
**Viz, 2004**
**ISBN 159116222X**
**$7.95**
**C**

Sai, the ghost of an ancient Go champion, trapped inside a Go game, informs this tale of Hikaru, who discovers the enchanted board in his grandfather's attic. Magically, the Go master fuses with Hikaru, and he becomes a master Go player. However, Sai has an ulterior motive: he wants to find a divine move so he can rest in peace.

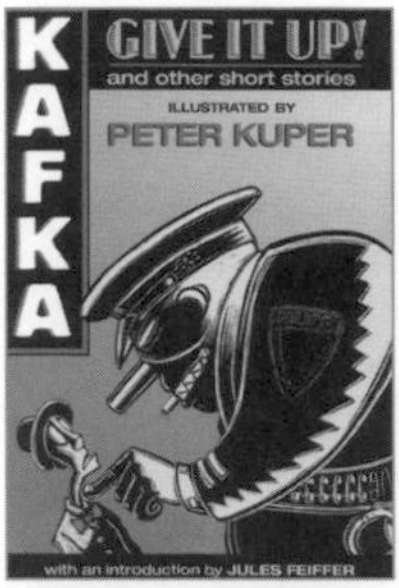
KAFKA
GIVE IT UP!
and other short stories
ILLUSTRATED BY
PETER KUPER
with an introduction by JULES FEIFFER

**Kafka, Franz & Peter Kuper**
***Give It Up! and Other Stories by Franz Kafka***
**NBM, 1995**
**ISBN 1561631256**
**$15.95**
**A**

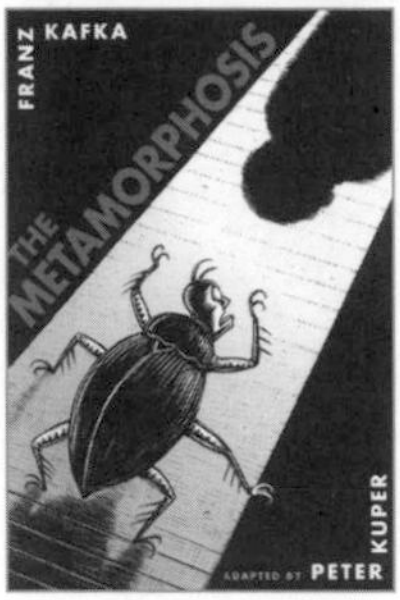
FRANZ KAFKA
THE METAMORPHOSIS
PETER KUPER

**Kafka, Franz & Peter Kuper**
***The Metamorphosis***
**Crown, 2003**
**ISBN 1400047951**
**$18.00**
**Y**

Named "Cartoonist of the Year" by *Rolling Stone* magazine in 1995, Kuper continues to create important comics. He adapts several of Kafka's works in *Give It Up!* In that volume's introduction, Jules Feiffer aptly compares these woodcut studies of Kafka's stories to jazz versions of Gershwin compositions. Kafka's sense of alienation is very real in these chilling and poignant woodcuts, which are interpretive rather than merely graphic. He then tackles Kafka's most famous tale, *The Metamorphosis,* utilizing a more traditional black-and-white line-drawing style, lending the classic story of alienation a twenty-first-century sensibility.

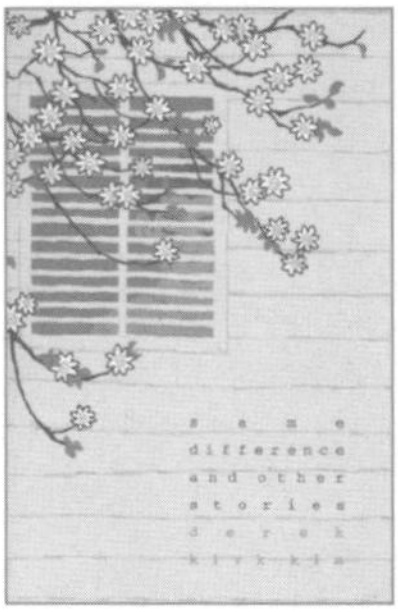

**Kim, Derek Kirk**
***Same Difference and Other Stories***
**Top Shelf Productions, 2004**
**ISBN 1891830570**
**$12.95**
**Y+**

This collection from young cartoonist Kim is stunning, displaying both a wide imagination and a variety of storytelling and cartooning skills. The title story focuses on twentysomethings Nancy and Simon, both with guilt on their consciences: Simon, for turning down a date with a friend because she was blind, and Nancy, for reading love letters meant for someone else and then answering them, giving the jilted ex-boyfriend hope. Through a series of credible coincidences, both Nancy and Simon make amends. What Kim does as well as anybody is portray the uneasy, vague, and lost feeling often experienced in late adolescence and early adulthood. The other stories included in the collection are shorter and cover high-school track, weed wacking, familial relationships, celebrity interviews, high school experiences, and autobiographical tales, all told in clear, humorous black and white pictures.

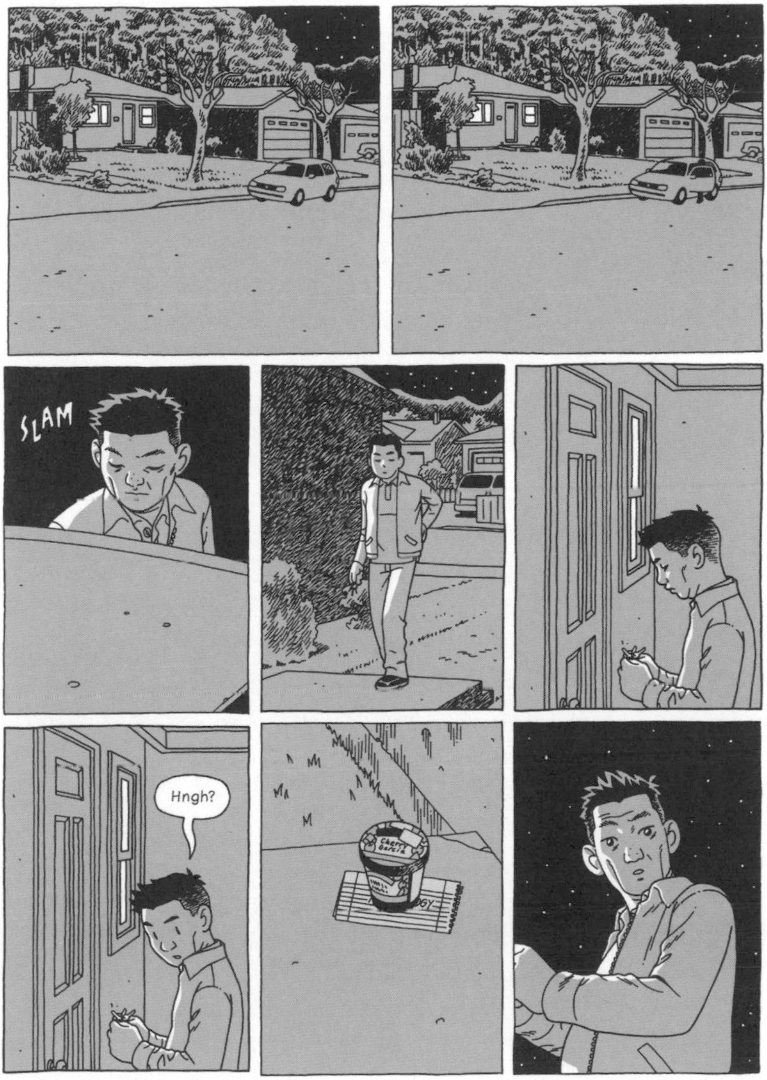
SLAM
Hngh?

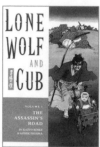

LONE WOLF AND CUB
VOLUME 1
THE ASSASSIN'S ROAD

**Koike, Kazuo & Goseki Kojima**
***Lone Wolf and Cub: The Assassin's Road***
**Dark Horse, 2000**
**ISBN 1569715025**
**$9.95**
**Y+**

SAMURAI EXECUTIONER

**Koike, Kazuo & Goseki Kojima**
***Samurai Executioner: When the Demon Knife Weeps***
**Dark Horse, 2004**
**ISBN 1593072074**
**$9.95**
**A**

*Lone Wolf and Cub* is a tale of a lone Samurai traveling with his child. Itto Ogami wanders the land after being cast out of Edo, awaiting the day he can take revenge on his enemies. Meticulously rendered and well researched, it was one of the first Japanese comics to reach these shores, and heavily influenced American cartoonists in the 1980s. All twenty-eight volumes have been published by Dark Horse Comics. *Samurai Executioner*'s lead character is the Shogun's Executioner, Decapitator Asaemon, a man who wields the "demon blade." Asa comes across an impressive cross-section of humanity, all of whom meet justice of one sort or another. Over a dozen volumes have been released. (The above citations are both for Volume 1 of the respective series.)

MAI
THE PSYCHIC GIRL
PERFECT COLLECTION
1

**Kudo, Kazuka**
***Mai the Psychic Girl: The Perfect Collection***
**Viz Media, 1996**
**ISBN 156931070X**
**$19.95**
**Y**

Teenagers will enjoy the realistic, absurd, and terrifying story of Mai, who appears like most fourteen-year-olds, except for her psychic abilities. Mai thinks her powers are useful primarily for jokes, but when her father is endangered, Mai realizes that her powers are serious, and must be used with purpose.

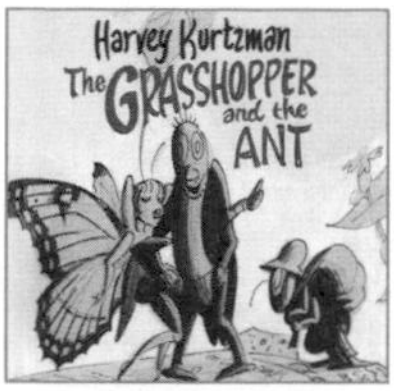
Harvey Kurtzman
The GRASSHOPPER and the ANT

**Kurtzman, Harvey**
***The Grasshopper and the Ant***
**Denis Kitchen Publishing, 2002**
**ISBN 0971008000**
**$25.00**
**Y**

One of the most influential cartoonists in American history, Kurtzman was the initial creative force behind *Mad* magazine. In this full-length story, originally published in *Esquire,* he talks both sides of the hippie revolution of the 1960s. The ant, toiling daily while living in quiet desperation, debates with the free-thinking grasshopper over life, love, and the pursuit of happiness.

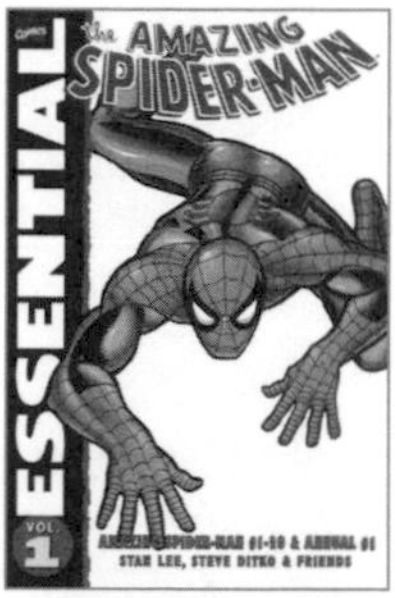
The AMAZING SPIDER-MAN
ESSENTIAL
VOL 1

**Lee, Stan & Steve Ditko**
***The Essential Spider-Man, Volume 1***
**Marvel Entertainment Group, 2002**
**ISBN 0785109889**
**$14.95**
**C**

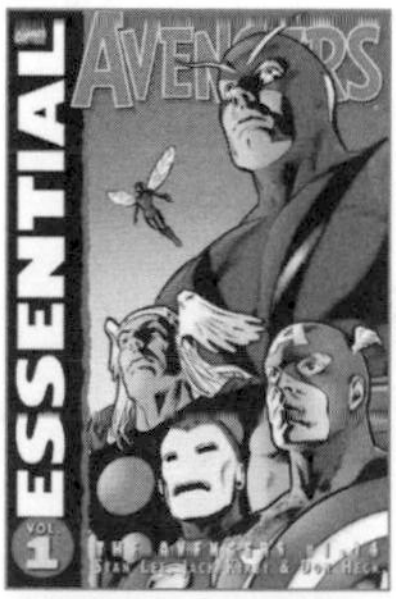
ESSENTIAL
VOL 1

**Lee, Stan & Jack Kirby, et al**
***The Essential Avengers, Volume 1***
**Marvel Entertainment Group, 1998**
**ISBN 0785107010**
**$14.95**
**C**

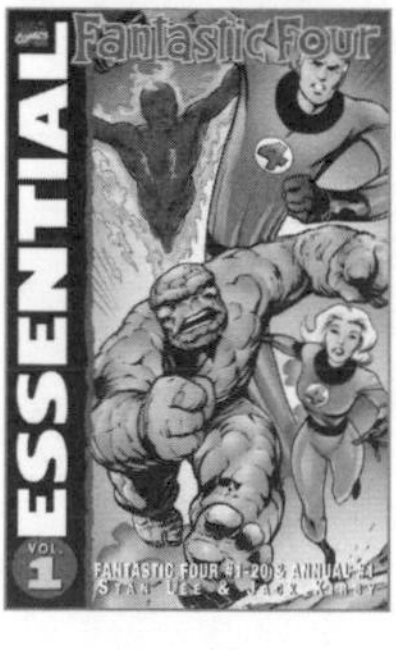
Fantastic Four
ESSENTIAL
VOL 1

**Lee, Stan & Jack Kirby, et al**
***The Essential Fantastic Four, Volume 1***
**Marvel Entertainment Group, 2005**
**ISBN 0785118284**
**$16.99**
**C**

The "Essential" volumes reprint a score of classic comics each in black-and-white. These volumes range from the Avengers—Marvel's answer to the Justice League, featuring their greatest heroes banded together in heartfelt, entertaining tales of heroism—to the Fantastic Four—the landmark heroes that kicked off the revitalization of the superhero genre in 1961—to Spider-Man—the defining modern hero caught between responsibility and temptation. Kirby's powerful art loses some verve without color, but Ditko's looks even better.

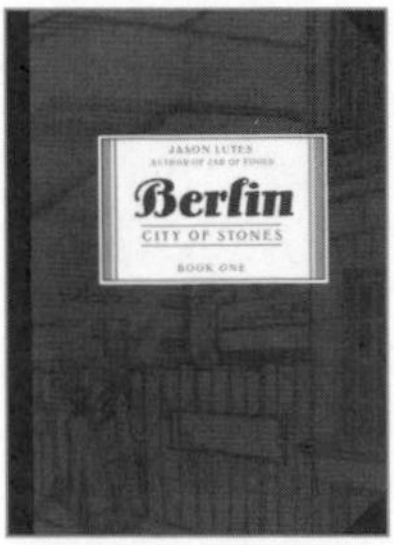
Berlin
CITY OF STONES

**Lutes, Jason**
***Berlin Book 1: City of Stones***
**Drawn and Quarterly, 2000**
**ISBN 1896597297**
**$19.95**
**Y+**

Lutes's first book, *Jar of Fools*—about a magician who has lost his confidence, but not his magic touch—was stellar. With *Berlin,* Lutes aims even higher. *City of Stones* is the first in a projected trilogy, and is set during the waning days of the Weimar Republic. The protagonists are Kurt, a journalist, and Marthe, an art student. Lutes has a feel for the personal and political turmoil in Germany following World War I. The illustrations are subtle and meditative.

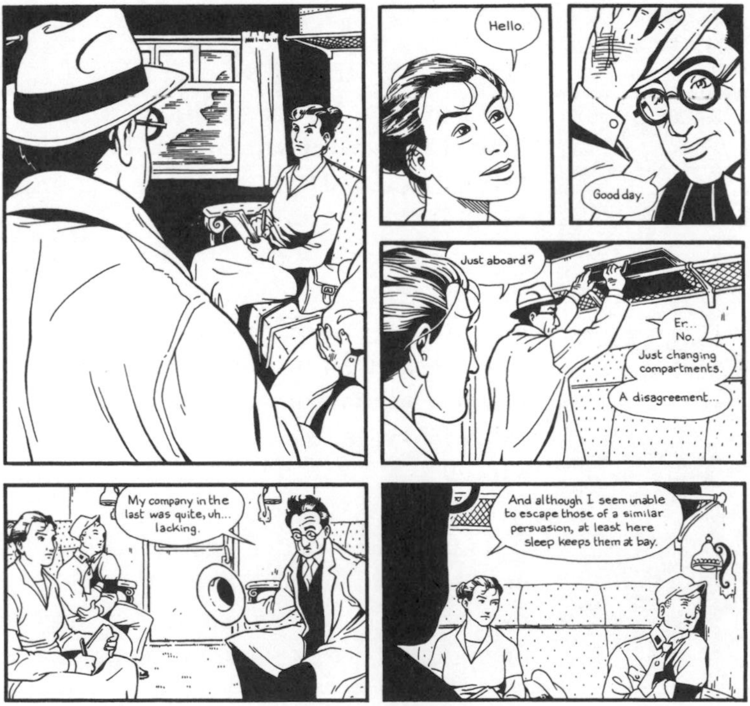
Hello.
Good day.
Just aboard?
Er... No.
Just changing compartments.
A disagreement...
My company in the last was quite, uh... lacking.
And although I seem unable to escape those of a similar persuasion, at least here sleep keeps them at bay.

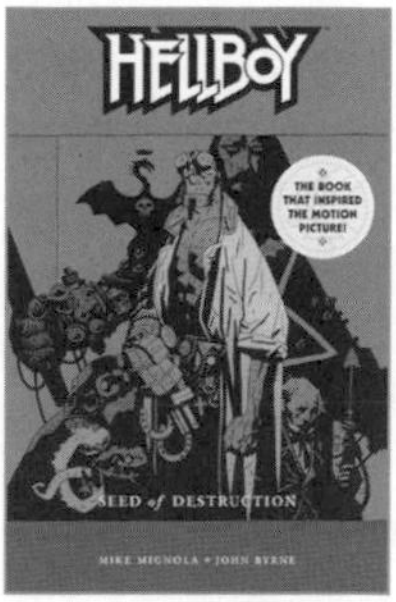
HELLBOY
SEED of DESTRUCTION

**Mignola, Mike**
***Hellboy: Seed of Destruction***
**Dark Horse, 2004**
**ISBN 1593070942**
**$17.95**
**Y**

Originally summoned from the depths of hell by the Nazis, Hellboy turned against them and became Earth's greatest paranormal investigator, determined to protect humanity from the forces of evil. A team composed of both mutants and humans aid him in his quest. Mignola's style is trend-setting: at once humorous, dramatic, arresting, and pleasing. The series has branched out into prose novels and movies. Other titles are: *Wake the Devil, The Chained Coffin and Others, The Right Hand of Doom,* and *Conqueror Worm.*

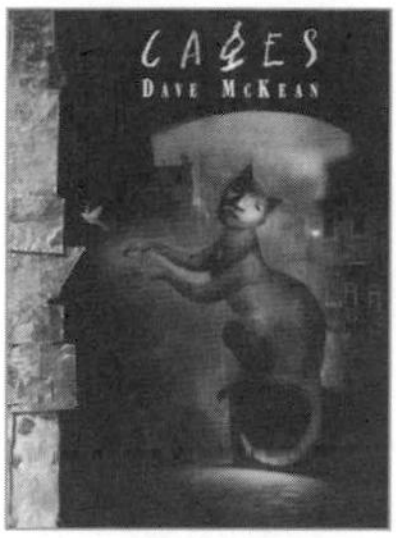
CAGES
DAVE McKEAN

**McKean, Dave**
***Cages***
**NBM, 2002**
**ISBN 1561633194**
**$50.00**
**A**

McKean is possibly the best known of the current artists creating work for adults, chiefly due to his prolific cover artwork in both "mature readers" comics such as *Sandman* and in books. *Cages* is the only work that McKean has written as well as drawn, and he uses the opportunity to present a dialogue on the hazards and rewards of creativity. *Cages* tells the story of three different artists: Leo Sabarsky, a painter in need of inspiration, Angel, a nightclub musician, who seems oblivious to to the adulation of his audience, and Jonathan Rush, whose novel *Cages* so enraged readers that he lives in captivity. How these characters break free of their mental cages forms the conflict of this book, which evolves into a meditation on creativity and godhood. The artwork is dynamic, and changes as McKean feels appropriate.

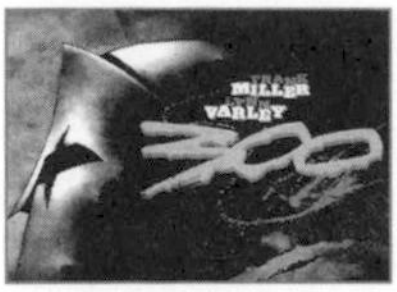
MILLER
VARLEY
300

**Miller, Frank**
***300***
**Dark Horse, 1999**
**ISBN 1569714029**
**$30.00**
**Y**

This treatment of the famous three hundred Spartan soldiers that took on the Persian Army is surprisingly well-served by Miller's hard-boiled style, honed on superhero comics and Miller's own *Sin City* books. An excellent use of modern genre conventions to tell a very old—and very compelling—story of bravery against impossible odds.

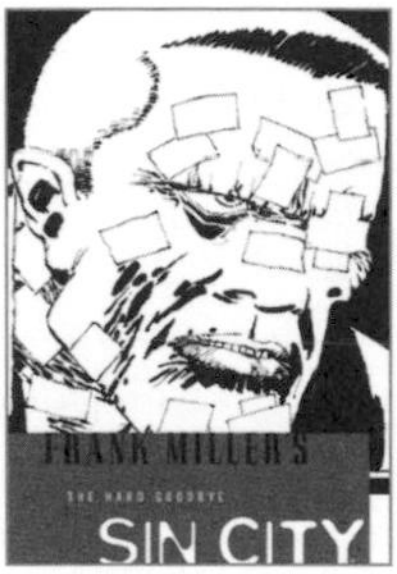
FRANK MILLER'S
SIN CITY

**Miller, Frank**
***Sin City: The Hard Goodbye***
**Dark Horse, 2005**
**ISBN 1593072937**
**$17.00**
**Y+**

Miller's tale of down-and-out Marv, who seems bigger than death, and who is determined to find a punish the murder of Goldie, a prostitute who showed him what love felt like, is rendered in exquisite black and white illustrations that suggest rather than tell. Other volumes in the series: *A Dame to Kill For, The Big Fat Kill, That Yellow Bastard, Family Values, Booze, Broads, & Bullets,* and *Hell and Back.* Several volumes, including *The Hard Goodbye,* were the the basis for the 2005 *Sin City* movie.

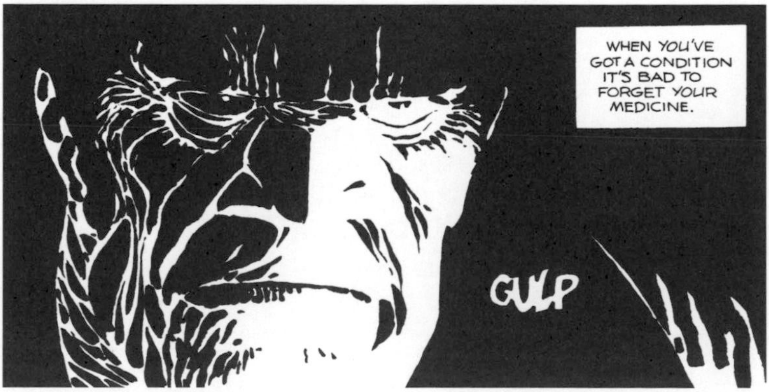
WHEN YOU'VE GOT A CONDITION IT'S BAD TO FORGET YOUR MEDICINE.
GULP

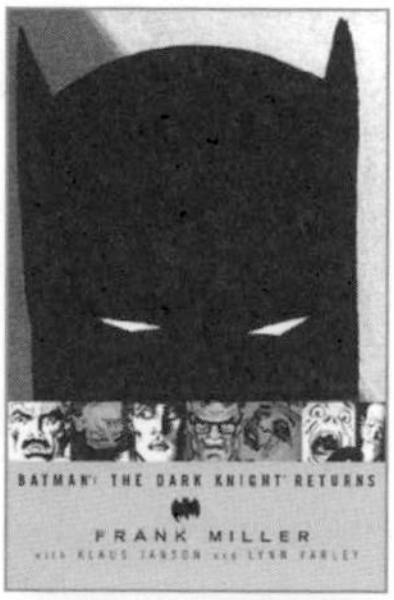
BATMAN: THE DARK KNIGHT RETURNS
FRANK MILLER

**Miller, Frank & Klaus Janson**
***Batman: The Dark Knight Returns***
**DC Comics, 2002**
**ISBN 156389341X**
**$24.95**
**Y**

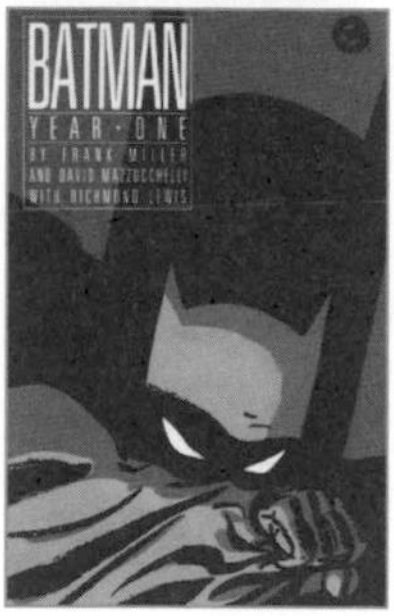
BATMAN
YEAR · ONE

**Miller, Frank & David Mazzucchelli**
***Batman: Year One***
**DC Comics, 1997**
**ISBN 0930289331**
**$9.95**
**Y**

These two volumes, along with the 1989 feature film, led a resurgence in popularity for this superhero icon. In *Dark Knight,* a fine study of vigilantes and violence, Batman at age 50 emerges from a ten-year retirement to save Gotham City from gang warfare and his nemesis, the Joker. In *Year One,* a partial source for the 2005 film *Batman Begins,* Miller and Mazzucchelli return to the origins of the character, and retell the first year of the life of the caped crusader after Bruce Wayne decides to don a costume and fight crime.

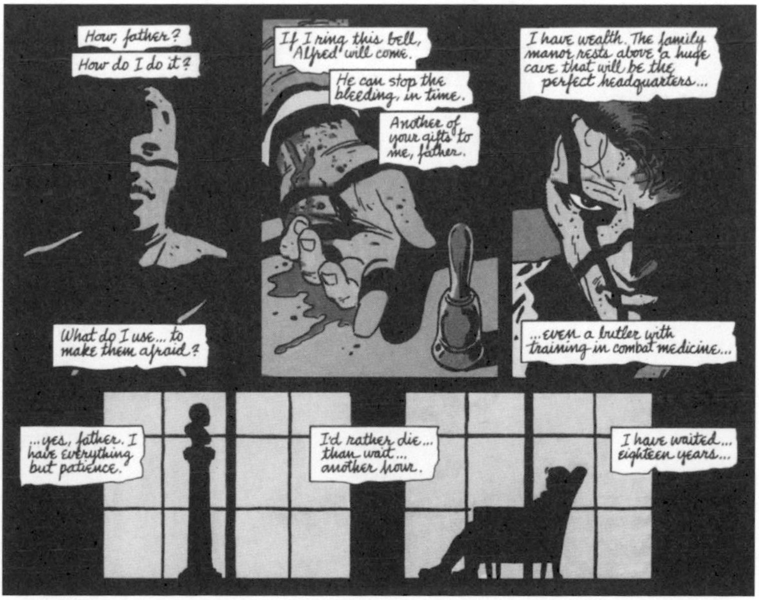
How, father?
How do I do it?
What do I use... to make them afraid?
If I ring this bell, Alfred will come.
He can stop the bleeding, in time.
Another of your gifts to me, father.
I have wealth. The family manor rests above a huge cave that will be the perfect headquarters...
...even a butler with training in combat medicine...
...yes, father. I have everything but patience.
I'd rather die... than wait... another hour.
I have waited... eighteen years...

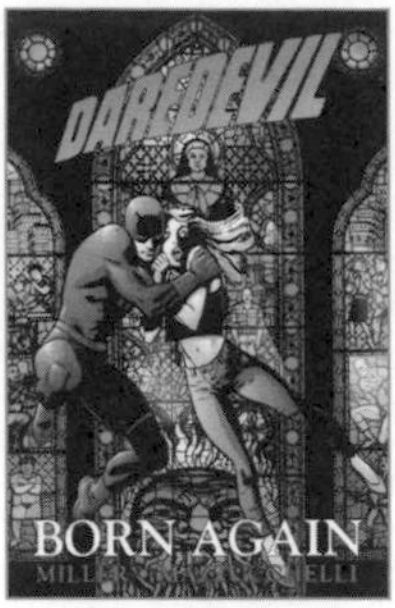
DAREDEVIL
BORN AGAIN

**Miller, Frank & David Mazzucchelli**
***Daredevil: Born Again***
**Marvel Entertainment Group, 1990**
**ISBN 0871352974**
**$17.95**
**Y+**

Miller and Mazzucchelli tell this pivotal story of Daredevil, a blind, acrobatic hero, who "sees" by using a radioactive "radar sense." Daredevil's enemy, the Kingpin, learns his secret identity and uses the information to destroy him. The loss teaches Daredevil at once how important and how irrelevant his secret identity is to him.

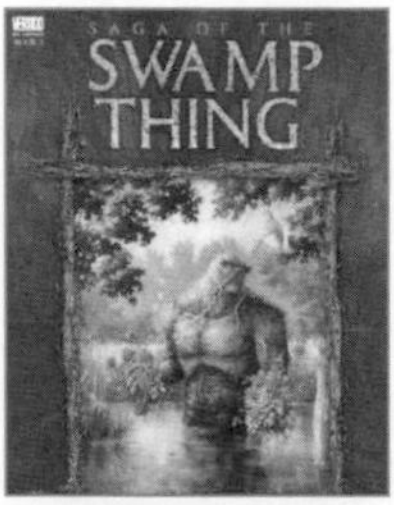
SAGA OF THE
SWAMP
THING

**Moore, Alan & Steve Bissette**
***The Saga of the Swamp Thing***
**DC Comics, 1998**
**ISBN 0930289226**
**$19.99**
**Y**

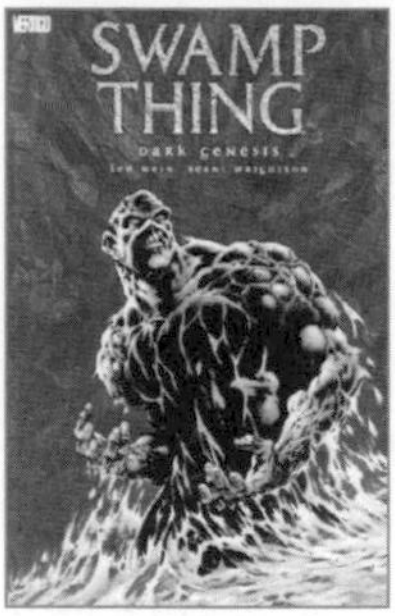
SWAMP
THING
dark genesis

**Wein, Len & Bernie Wrightson**
***Swamp Thing: Dark Genesis***
**DC Comics, 2002**
**ISBN 1563890445**
**$19.95**
**C**

*The Swamp Thing* comic explored what constituted humanity through the tale of biologist Alec Holland, transformed into a swamp creature by an explosion. With no hope of humanity left in his body, the Swamp Thing begins his journey back. *Dark Genesis* reprints the early *Swamp Thing* stories from the 1970s, with eerie and probing artwork from Wrightson and entertaining stories from Wein. *The Saga of the Swamp Thing* sees Moore and Bissette building on Wein and Wrightson's foundation to explore issues of the human condition in greater depth.

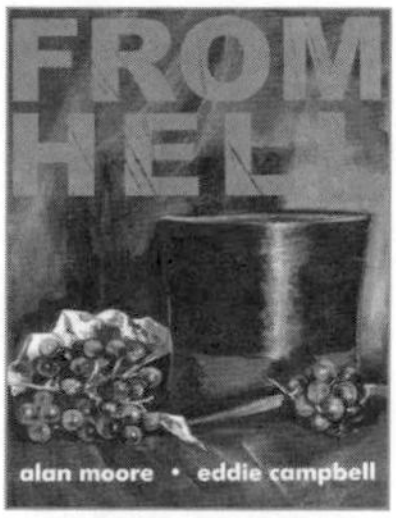
FROM HELL
alan moore • eddie campbell

**Moore, Alan & Eddie Campbell**
***From Hell***
**Top Shelf Productions, 2004**
**ISBN 0958578346**
**$35.00**
**A**

Moore and Campbell have created a treat for horror readers, as they present this "melodrama in sixteen parts," which thoroughly investigates the Jack the Ripper murder spree in late-19th-century London. Meticulously researched and documented, *From Hell* provides atmosphere for this horrific serial murder. Campbell's scratchy drawings are riveting. This is fiction, but it is almost history. (See also Rick Geary's *Jack the Ripper*.)

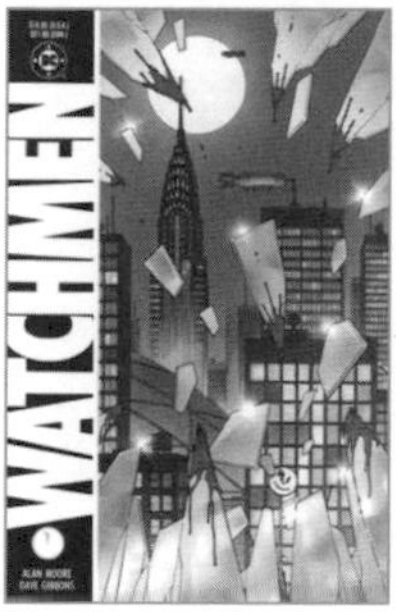
WATCHMEN

**Moore, Alan & Dave Gibbons**
***Watchmen***
**Warner Books, 1995**
**ISBN 0930289234**
**$19.99**
**Y**

Moore and Gibbons offer what many consider to be the ultimate superhero story in the form of a meditation on time and the burdens of power. In a fantasy world, Richard Nixon never resigned after Watergate, but all the superheroes were outlawed. Those with normal (acrobatic, scientific) abilities went into hiding; Dr. Manhattan, a man atomically empowered by an explosion, was exempted, as he worked for the government. The disappearance of Dr. Manhattan brings the lesser heroes/vigilantes out of hiding, and humanity must face the result in this compelling examination of how the presence of super-powered individuals can truly change the world.

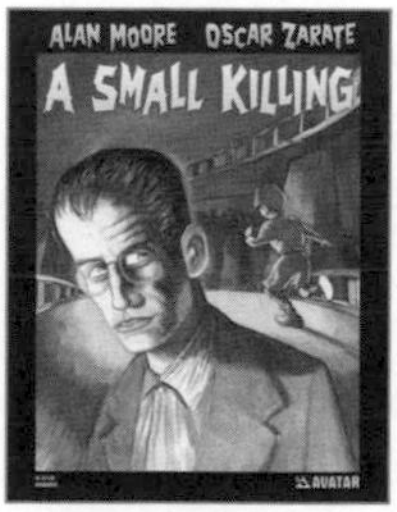
ALAN MOORE OSCAR ZARATE
A SMALL KILLING

**Moore, Alan & Oscar Zarate**
***A Small Killing***
**Avatar Press, 2003**
**ISBN 1592910092**
**$16.95**
**Y**

Who is the child following artist-turned-adman Timothy Holly?

When Timothy learns the answer to that question, he must return to childhood and choose maturity as he grows this time.

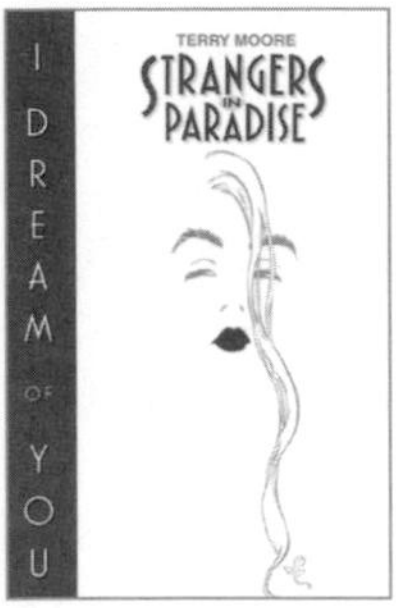
TERRY MOORE
STRANGERS IN PARADISE
I DREAM OF YOU

**Moore, Terry**
***Strangers in Paradise: I Dream of You***
**Abstract Studio, 1996**
**ISBN 1892597012**
**$16.95**
**Y+**

The serial *Strangers in Paradise* tells the stories of twentysomethings Katchoo, explosive and independent, and Francine, whose idea of a day well spent is returning a bird's egg to its nest. When newcomer David comes between them in this volume, there's not only jealousy and rejection in the mix, but Katchoo's dark past, which David somehow brings with him. While *Strangers in Paradise* is noteworthy for its fine characterizations and human dramas, it is also a good example of how the comics medium can merge with other forms; some of the book appears as prose, and the title, "I Dream of You," is a song. A good book for those who don't read comics, an even better book for those who do. Other titles include *High School!, Immortal Enemies, It's a Good Life, Love Me Tender,* and *Sanctuary.* Collections are also available in digest size.

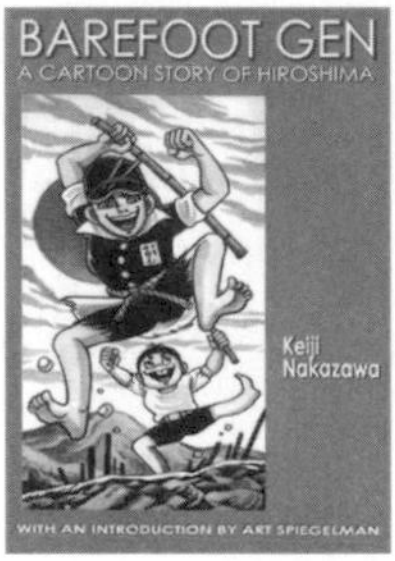
BAREFOOT GEN
A CARTOON STORY OF HIROSHIMA
Keiji Nakazawa
WITH AN INTRODUCTION BY ART SPIEGELMAN

**Nakazawa, Keiji**
***Barefoot Gen: A Cartoon Story of Hiroshima***
**Last Gasp, 2004**
**ISBN 0867196025**
**$14.95**
**A**

The clear cartoons in this story convey an important history of World War II in a very accessible format. Originally published in Japan, this series influenced Art Spiegelman, who wrote the introduction.

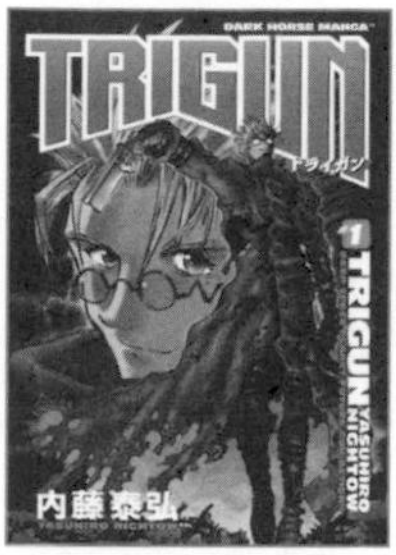
DARK HORSE MANGA
TRIGUN
1 TRIGUN
YASUHIRO NIGHTOW
内藤泰弘

**Nightow, Yasuhiro**
***Trigun Volume 1***
**Dark Horse, 2003**
**ISBN 1593070527**
**$14.95**
**Y**

This book, the first of several volumes, mixes comedy, science fiction, and the Old West. Protagonist Vash has a sixty-billion-dollar double bounty on his head. Nightow's style is cinematic and sincere in this fast-paced thriller.

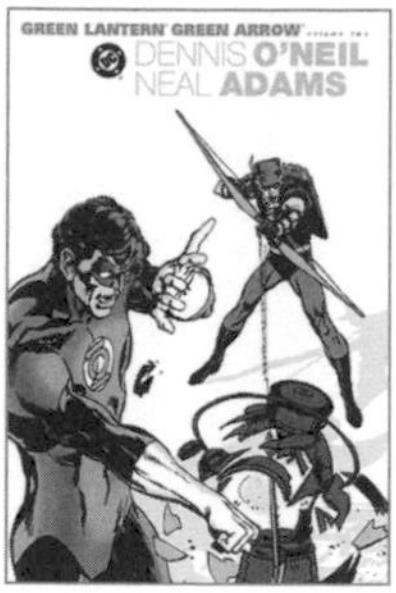
GREEN LANTERN GREEN ARROW
DENNIS O'NEIL
NEAL ADAMS

**O'Neil, Dennis & Neal Adams, et al**
***Green Lantern/Green Arrow Volume 2***
**DC Comics, 2004**
**ISBN 1401202306**
**$12.95**
**Y**

In this chapter of the *Green Lantern/Green Arrow* series, the heroes confront drug abuse and racism in groundbreaking stories originally published in the 1970s. Though the stories may seem dated to some, they are important parts of superhero comics history.

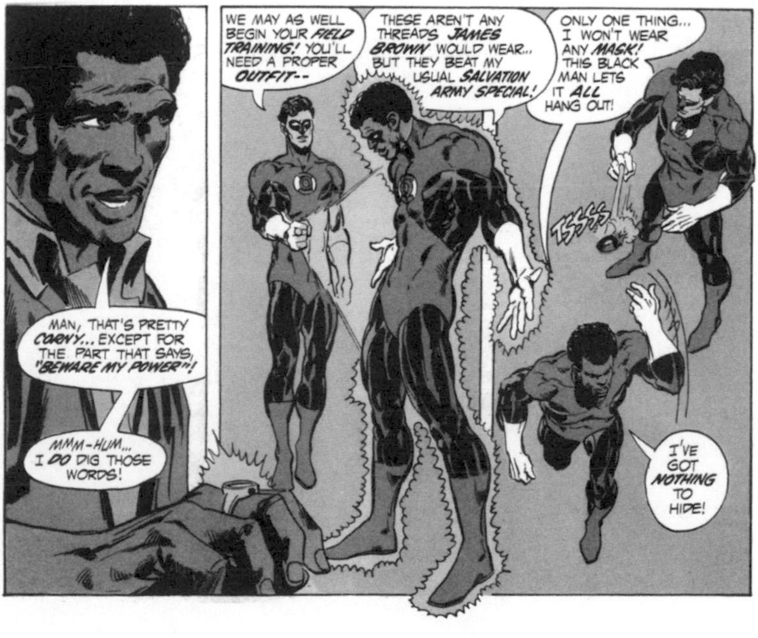
MAN, THAT'S PRETTY CORNY... EXCEPT FOR THE PART THAT SAYS, "BEWARE MY POWER"!
MMM-HUM... I DO DIG THOSE WORDS!
WE MAY AS WELL BEGIN YOUR FIELD TRAINING! YOU'LL NEED A PROPER OUTFIT--
THESE AREN'T ANY THREADS JAMES BROWN WOULD WEAR... BUT THEY BEAT MY USUAL SALVATION ARMY SPECIAL!
ONLY ONE THING... I WON'T WEAR ANY MASK! THIS BLACK MAN LETS IT ALL HANG OUT!
TSSSS
I'VE GOT NOTHING TO HIDE!

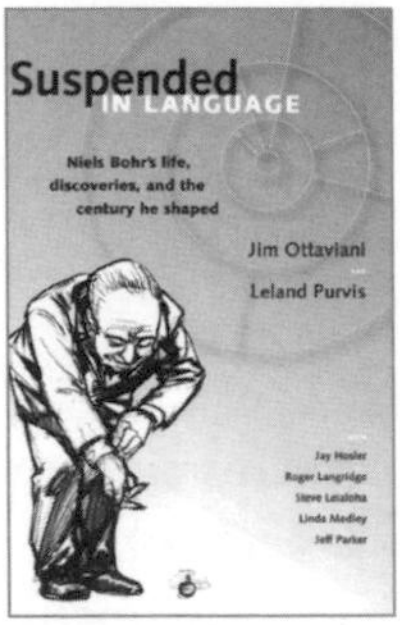
Suspended
IN LANGUAGE
Niels Bohr's life, discoveries, and the century he shaped
Jim Ottaviani
Leland Purvis

**Ottaviani, Jim, with Leland Purvis**
***Suspended in Language: Neils Bohr's Life, Discoveries, and the Century He Shaped***
**G.T. Labs, 2004**
**ISBN 0966010655**
**$24.95**
**Y**

Ottaviani's earlier books, Fallout and Two-Fisted Science, both earned high praise. Here he examines the life of Bohr, the physicist who greatly influenced Albert Einstein and founded quantum mechanics.

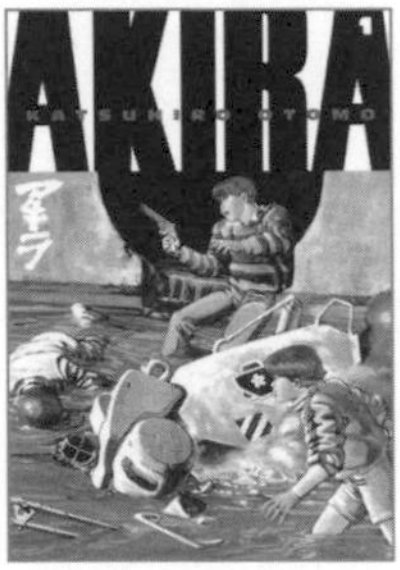
AKIRA 1
KATSUHIRO OTOMO

**Otomo, Katsuhiro**
***Akira***
**Dark Horse, 2000**
**ISBN 1569714983**
**$24.95**
**Y**

Set in the year 2030, thirty-eight years after World War III, *Akira* tells the story of two motorbiking teenagers who encounter a child with the features of an old man. When one of the teens experiences supernatural powers that threaten him, both teens become involved in a war between two agencies, both intent on saving the world. With artwork that seems bigger than the page it's drawn on, *Akira* is a book that engrosses and involves the reader. This is a multi-book series.

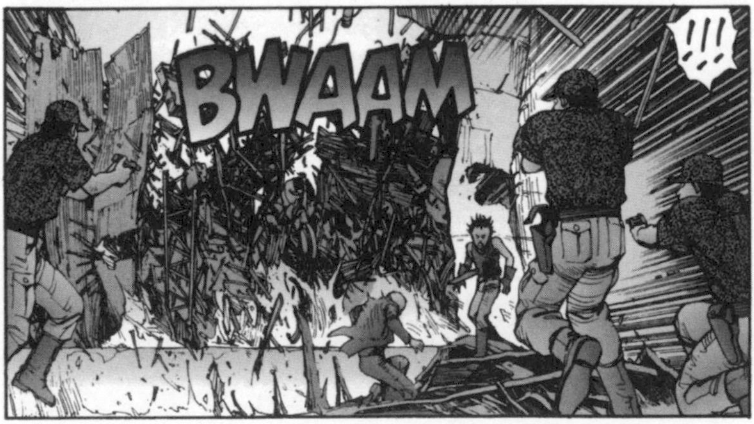
!!!
BWAAM

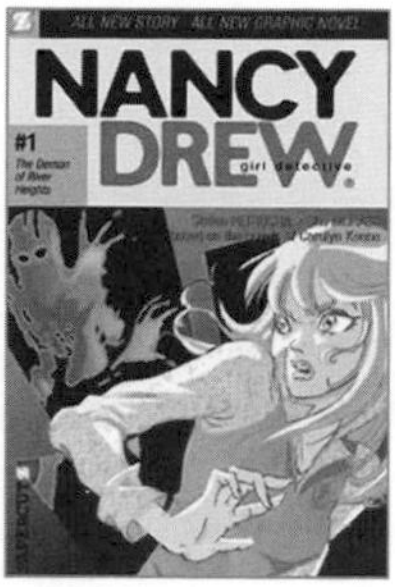
NANCY DREW
#1
girl detective

**Petrucha, Stefan & Shi Murase**
***Nancy Drew: The Demon of River Heights***
**Papercutz/NBM, 2005**
**ISBN 1597070041**
**$12.95**
**C**

One of the traditions in comics storytelling is adaptation of classics into comics form. Now Papercutz (a division of this book's publisher, NBM) has developed new stories for Nancy Drew in a series of graphic novels with artwork reminiscent of the manga style. In *The Demon of River Heights,* Nancy and friends Bess and George stumble onto a mystery while helping some college students make a film. Nancy is a strong complex character imbued with skills and weaknesses, and humor builds dramatic tension, bringing the story to a satisfying conclusion.

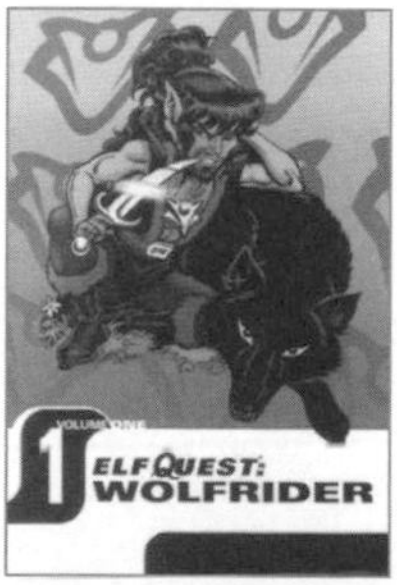
1
ELFQUEST:
WOLFRIDER

**Pini, Wendy & Richard**
***ElfQuest: Wolfrider Volume 1***
**DC Comics, 2003**
**ISBN 1401201318**
**$9.95**
**Y**

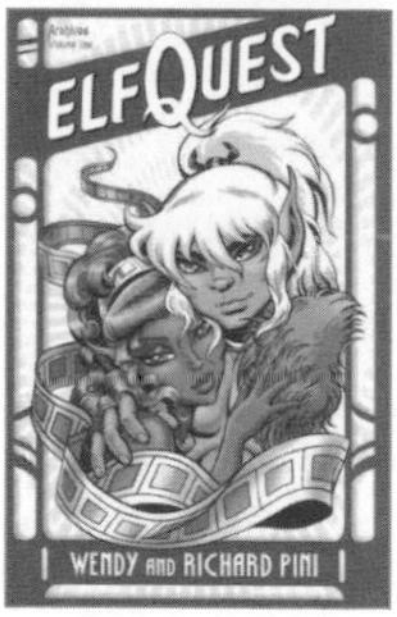
ELFQUEST
WENDY AND RICHARD PINI

**Pini, Wendy & Richard**
***ElfQuest: Archives Volume 1***
**DC Comics, 2003**
**ISBN 1401201288**
**$49.95**
**Y**

Originally self-published by this husband-and-wife team, this story of a race of elves searching for their true homeland on a world very much like Earth grown into a sprawling, epic tale. Inspired in part by European, Norse, and Native-American mythologies, the series focuses on Chief Cutter, who struggles to build a stable society. DC has republished the entire series in two formats, in an inexpensive digest size, which reproduces the series chronologically, and in the more expensive, "archive" format, which presents the series as it first appeared in a high-quality, permanent edition.

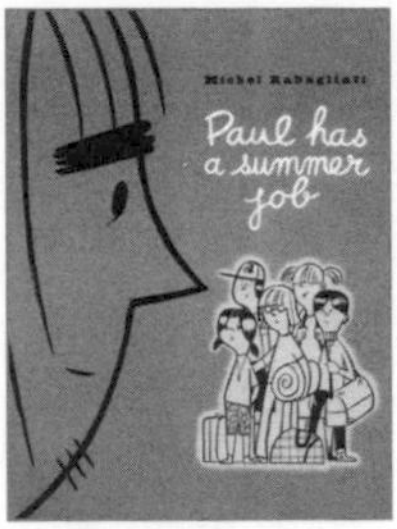
Paul has a summer job

**Rabagliati, Michel**
***Paul Has a Summer Job***
**Drawn and Quarterly, 2003**
**ISBN 1896597548**
**$16.95**
**Y+**

In a fit of rage, Paul quits high school and starts working for a printer. When that doesn't work out, he accepts a job as a camp counselor. However, Paul is poorly prepared to supervise children. Through relationships with both a blind camper and his co-counselor, Paul begins the slow journey toward maturity. Rabagliati's artistic style is unadorned, humorous, and compassionate. Other Paul books include *Paul Moves Out.*

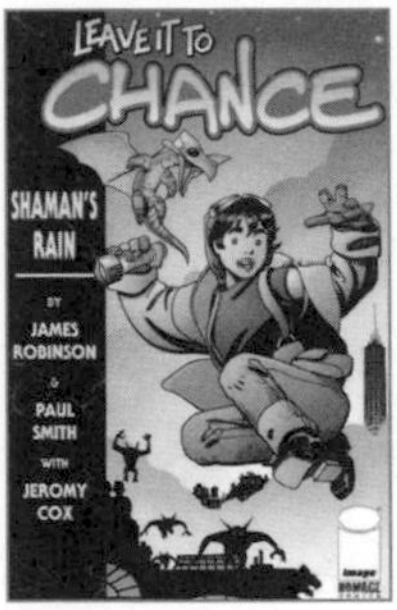
Leave it to
CHANCE
SHAMAN'S RAIN
BY JAMES ROBINSON & PAUL SMITH WITH JEROMY COX

**Robinson, James & Paul Smith**
***Leave It to Chance Volume 1: Shaman's Rain***
**Image Comics, 2002**
**ISBN 1582402531**
**$14.95**
**Y**

Fourteen-year-old Chance wants to follow in her father's footsteps and become a mage. When she approaches her father telling him it's time for her apprenticeship to begin, he refuses, saying it's too dangerous, that when she bears a son the son will become the mage that Chance's father won't let her become. When, in Nancy Drew fashion, Chance unknowingly stumbles onto the mystery that her father is working on, she enters the terrifying world of magic. Other books in the delightfully charming adventure series include *Trick or Treat* and *Monster Madness.*

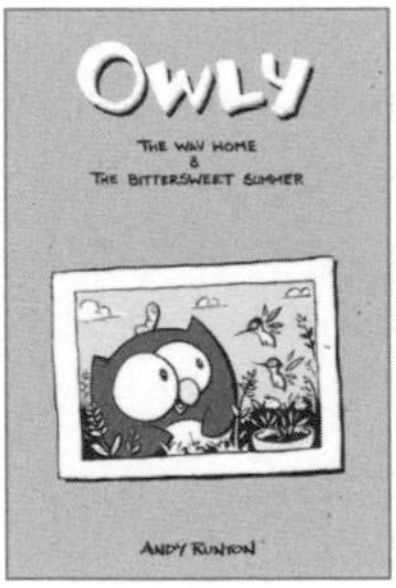
OWLY
THE WAY HOME & THE BITTERSWEET SUMMER
ANDY RUNTON

**Runton, Andy**
***Owly Volume 1: The Way Home***
***& The Bittersweet Summer***
**Top Shelf Productions, 2004**
**ISBN 1891830627**
**$10.00**
**C**

This little book presents two charming wordless stories about a young owl in search of companionship and adventure, as

Owly befriends a worm and a pair of hummingbirds. When the birds migrate south for the winter, the young owl is disconsolate. When he learns that the birds will return in the spring, he is overjoyed. Runton's artwork is warm and poignant, and the small, black-and-white illustration style matches the book's content perfectly. Especially appropriate for young children. Also available is Volume 2: *Just a Little Blue.*

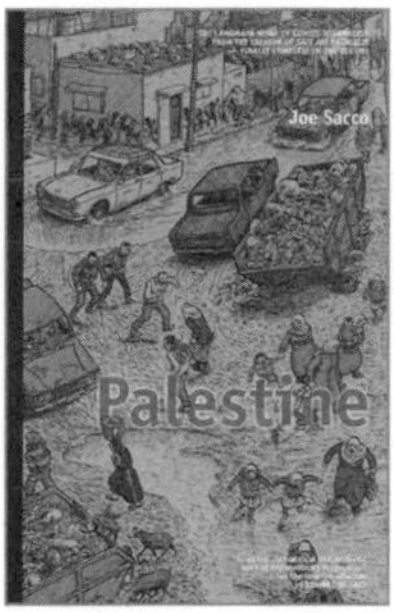
Joe Sacco
Palestine

**Sacco, Joe**
***Palestine***
**Fantagraphics Books, 2001**
**ISBN 156097432X**
**$24.95**
**Y**

A comics journalist whose style is influenced by Tom Wolfe and Robert Crumb, Sacco has worked for *Newsweek* and received a Guggenheim. This book details his experiences during visits to the West Bank and Gaza Strip, and the information is presented in a clear, articulate manner on a critical topic. Also recommended is Sacco's *Safe Area Goradze: the War in Eastern Bosnia, 1992-95* and *The Fixer.*

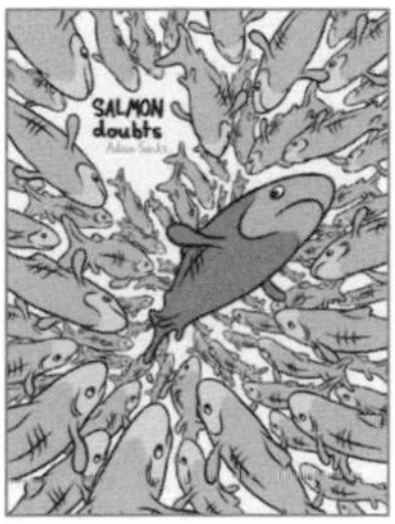
SALMON
doubts

**Sacks, Adam**
***Salmon Doubts***
**Alternative Comics, 2004**
**ISBN 1891867717**
**$14.95**
**Y**

Young Geoff, a salmon with a philosophical bent, melds with the group with some difficulty. When he learns that, for most salmon in his school, life consists of following preset social patterns, he breaks with convention by refusing to swim upstream, demonstrating to the other salmon that life does consist of choices. Sacks has created an entertaining, pleasurable parable about questioning the predetermined life.

YOJIMBO
BOOK ONE

**Sakai, Stan**
***Usagi Yojimbo Book 1: The Ronin***
**Fantagraphics Books, 1997**
**ISBN 0930193350**
**$15.95**
**C**

Japan in the seventeenth century was a time of great political unrest, with the samurai as the ruling class. Recalling western movies such as *Shane,* Usagi Yojimbo is a wandering masterless samurai for hire. Sakai deftly portrays the protagonist (a rabbit samurai) as honorable and tortured while somehow wrapping the character in an engaging, lively, and mildly humorous tale. This is an ongoing series with sixteen books in print.

PERSEPOLIS
MARJANE SATRAPI

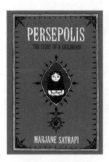

**Satrapi, Marjane**
***Persepolis: The Story of A Childhood***
**Pantheon Books, 2004**
**ISBN 037571457X**
**$11.95**
**Y**

Satrapi, a successful children's book writer, recounts the story of growing up under the repressive Iranian regime. The childlike illustrations counter the pervasive oppression. Also recommended is the second installment in Satrapi's life story, *Persepolis 2: The Story of a Return.*

CLYDE
FANS
BOOK·1

**Seth**
***Clyde Fans Book 1***
**Drawn and Quarterly, 2004**
**ISBN 189659784X**
**$19.95**
**Y+**

One of the modern masters of comic art, Seth has created a completely involving story of the seemingly mundane life of two brothers and their fan manufacturing company. Simon, a failure in the eyes of his brother Abraham because he can't seal the deal, studies sales manuals without success. Meditative and thought provoking, this book explores the relationship between two brothers. The first of a projected trilogy.

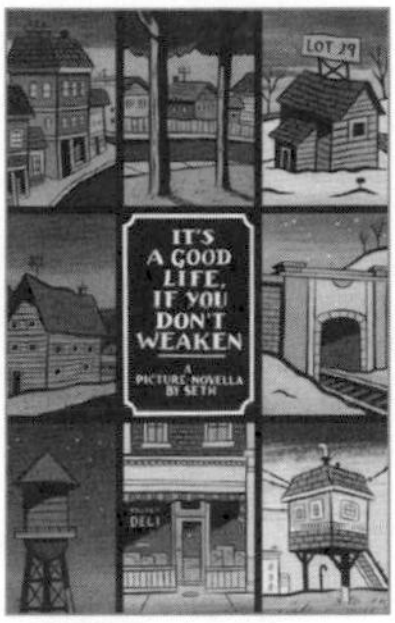
IT'S A GOOD LIFE, IF YOU DON'T WEAKEN

**Seth**
***It's a Good Life if You Don't Weaken***
**Drawn & Quarterly, 2003**
**ISBN 189659770X**
**$19.95**
**A**

This bittersweet autobiographical tale tells of Seth's attempts at maturity as he drifts in and out of relationships while searching for information about "Kalo," a cartoonist who placed a piece with the *New Yorker* magazine in the 1950s. The pacing is medative, and the book is kindly drawn. While readers might squirm at Seth's self-delusions, the conclusion teaches us of the redemptive power of art.

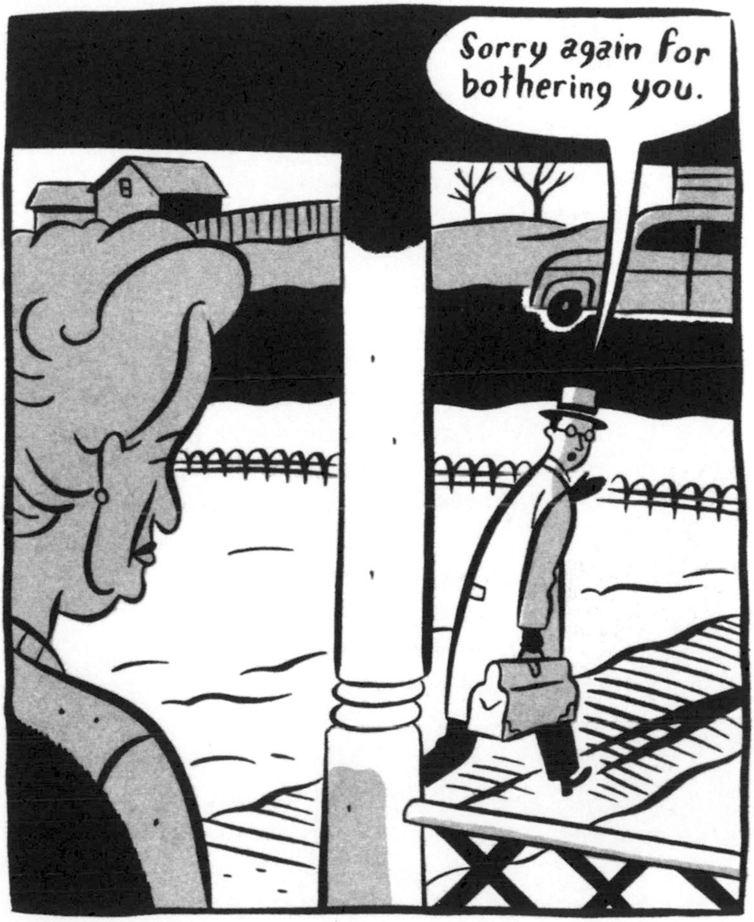
Sorry again for bothering you.

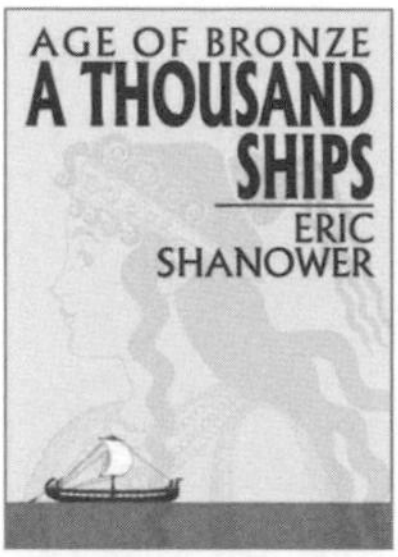
AGE OF BRONZE
A THOUSAND SHIPS
ERIC SHANOWER

**Shanower, Eric**
***Age of Bronze: A Thousand Ships***
**Image Comics, 2001**
**ISBN 1582402000**
**$19.95**
**Y**

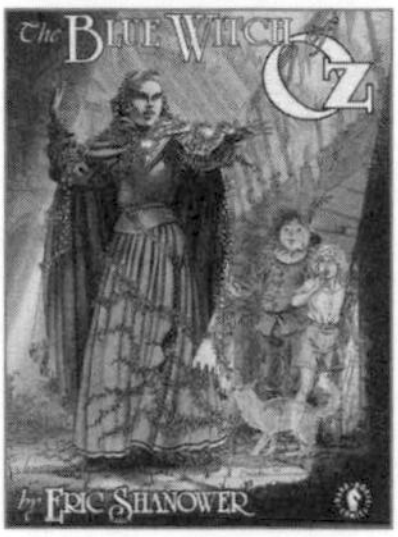
The BLUE WITCH of OZ
by ERIC SHANOWER

**Shanower, Eric**
***The Blue Witch of Oz***
**Dark Horse Comics, 1993**
**ISBN 1878574442**
**$9.95**
**C**

Shanower has adapted many of the L. Frank Baum *Wizard of Oz* stories into comics. The books are beautiful, with soft colors, and the dialogue is crisp. This is an excellent addition to Oz lore, which gains in popularity as time passes. Other titles include *The Enchanted Apples of Oz, The Forgotten Forest of Oz, The Giant Garden of Oz, The Ice King of Oz, Paradox in Oz* (with Edward Einhorn), *The Runaway in Oz* (with John R. Neill), and *The Secret Island of Oz.* Shanower has taken on an ambitious project with *Age of Bronze:* a seven-volume retelling of the Trojan War. Meticulously researched, this book tries to treat the war as history rather than mythology, and renders the world with a bronze look while exploring the social, political, and sexual aspects of the most famous war in Western literature. The sequel volume is also available entitled *Sacrifice.*

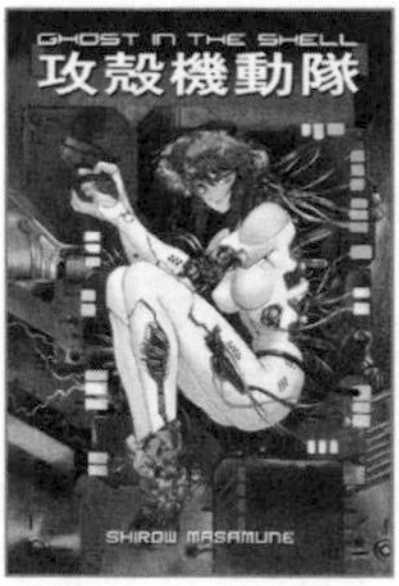
GHOST IN THE SHELL
攻殻機動隊
SHIROW MASAMUNE

**Shirow, Masamune**
***Ghost in the Shell***
**Dark Horse, 2004**
**ISBN 1593072287**
**$24.95**
**Y+**

Set in 2029, this futuristic story depicts a society dependant on cyborgs (part human, part machine) for military actions. Led by Major Kusanagi, a female, the crew investigate espionage and political alliances in a society fraught with criminals and terrorists who illegally copy the souls of human slaves, creating black-market cyborgs. Also available: *Ghost in the Shell 2.* This story was also the basis of a seminal anime film.

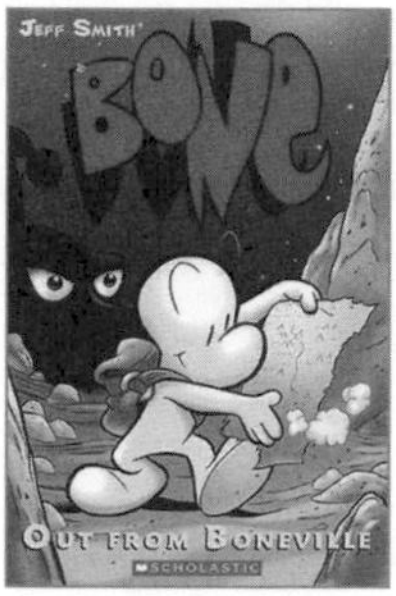
JEFF SMITH'
BONE
OUT FROM BONEVILLE
SCHOLASTIC

**Smith, Jeff**
***Bone: Out From Boneville***
**Scholastic, 2005**
**ISBN 0439706238**
**$18.95**
**C**

Smith's *Bone* series ran in nine volumes from 1991-2004 under his own imprint, Cartoon Books, and won both national and international awards. Reprinted by Scholastic in color beginning in 2005, it tells the story of three Bone cousins lost in a pre-technological world caught up in a battle for control of the valley. By turns dramatic and humorous, Smith's skills are consummate, and the books have delighted readers of all ages. *Out from Boneville* begins the story as the three cousins are run out of Boneville, only to find they are far from any world they know and have few skills which with to survive. Other books in the series are: *The Great Cow Race, Eyes of the Storm, The Dragonslayer, Rock Jaw Master of the Eastern Border, Old Man's Cave, Ghost Circles, Treasure Hunters,* and *Crown of Thorns.* Cartoon Books also collected the entire series as one huge book entitled *Bone: One Volume.*

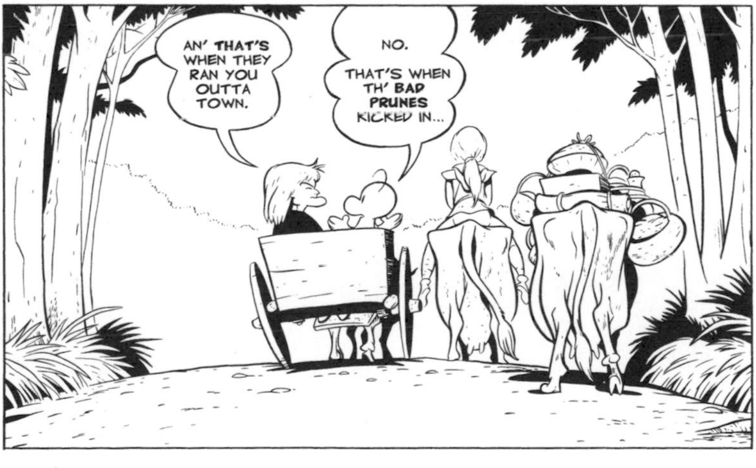
AN' THAT'S WHEN THEY RAN YOU OUTTA TOWN.
NO.
THAT'S WHEN TH' BAD PRUNES KICKED IN...

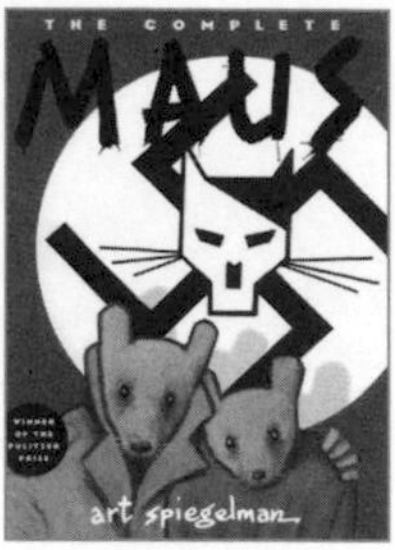
THE COMPLETE
MAUS
art spiegelman

**Spiegelman, Art**
***Maus: A Survivor's Tale***
**Pantheon Books, 1996**
**ISBN 0679406417**
**$35.00**
**Y**

This book collects both *Maus* volumes, *My Father Bleeds History* and *And Here My Troubles Began.* Volume 1 describes Spiegelman's father Vladek's struggle to survive concentration camps during World War II. Volume 2 relates the trials of Spiegelman's parents as they build a life in America. Awarded the Pulitzer prize in 1992, *Maus* is in part a meditation on fame, success, and an exploration into familial responsibility, as Spiegelman asks what his debt is to his deranged father, and whether or not commercial success is rewarding if the price is lost autonomy. Arguably the most important piece of comic art ever published.

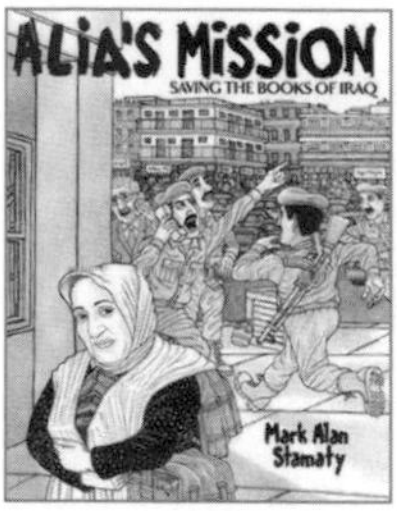
ALIA'S MISSION
SAVING THE BOOKS OF IRAQ
Mark Alan Stamaty

**Stamaty, Mark Alan**
***Alia's Mission: Saving the Books of Iraq***
**Alfred A. Knopf, 2004**
**ISBN 0375832173**
**$12.95**
**C**

This novel intended for young readers tells the true story of Alia, chief librarian of the Basra central library. When Alia realizes that the war makes the library vulnerable, she alerts the government. When government officials ignore her concerns, Alia takes matters into her own hands, and secretly removes some of the books from the library and stores them in her home. When looters break into the library, Alia enlists the aid of her friends in removing more books from the library. As the story ends, readers learn of Alia's role in the building of the new library.

**Stevens, Karl**
***Guilty***
**Karl Stevens Publishing, 2005**
**ISBN 0976459507**
**$10.00**
**Y+**

Former lovers Ingrid and Mark meet by chance at the bus stop, then learn that they are both employed at the same art museum in Cambridge, Massachusetts. As both of them flirt with the idea of rekindling their battered relationship, the reader is able to picture both sides of the story. Stevens's line work is sure, his sense of human relationships subtle, and his reach is deft.

THE GOLEM'S
MIGHTY SWING
BY JAMES STURM

**Sturm, James**
***The Golem's Mighty Swing***
**Drawn and Quarterly, 2001**
**ISBN 1896597459**
**$16.95**
**Y**

This book focuses on a traveling Jewish team during the early days of baseball. Sturm delivers a bittersweet tale that will appeal to readers of baseball and Jewish history.

He towers over batters. The pitcher's mound may as well be Mt. Sinai...
as he *hurls* fastballs like *lightning* bolts from its summit!

Yu-Gi-Oh!
Kazuki Takahashi
volume 1

**Takahashi, Kazuki**
***Yu-Gi-Oh! Volume 1***
**Viz Media, 2003**
**ISBN 1569319030**
**$7.95**
**C**

Solitary tenth-grader Yugi excelled at games, but when he solved the Millennium Puzzle, he awakened forces of evil many thousands of years old, and created a world full of wagers with possibly disastrous consequences. Taken from the popular TV show of the same name, Takahashi's storytelling and artwork match the story's themes perfectly.

The Tale of One Bad Rat
by
Bryan Talbot

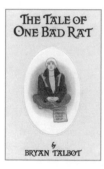

**Talbot, Bryan**
***The Tale of One Bad Rat***
**Dark Horse, 1995**
**ISBN 1569710775**
**$14.95**
**Y+**

The title of this affecting book is a nod to Beatrix Potter, whose books inspire protagonist Helen in her flight from an abusive father. As she flees, Helen follows the trail of Potter in an effort to gain the strength to move on, as the abuse has ended. After a joust with the police, Helen lands a job at an inn once visited by Potter, and over time reaches the inner resolve necessary to confront her parents and take control of her life.

The Bloody Streets of Paris
Jacques Tardi
Leo Malet

**Tardi, Jaques, with Leo Malet**
***The Bloody Streets of Paris***
**ibooks, 2003**
**ISBN 0743474481**
**$17.95**
**Y+**

Tardi's artful and atmospheric adaptation of Malet's 1942 detective novel introduces Nestor Burma, a world-class detective weary under Nazi rule. When a friend and colleague is assassinated, Burma must find the responsible party. His search leads him into the hands of French Nazi sympathizers, as we as the Gestapo. Gritty and realistic.

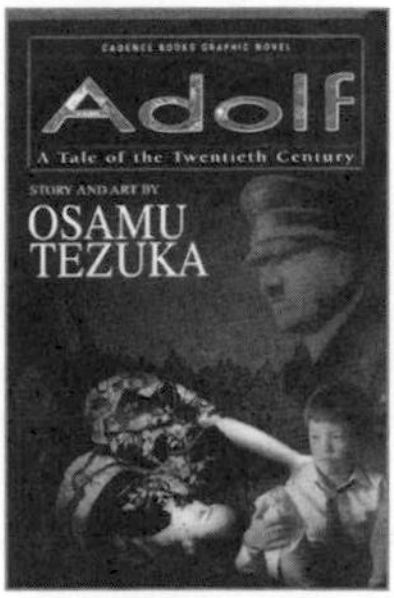
Adolf
A Tale of the Twentieth Century
STORY AND ART BY
OSAMU TEZUKA

**Tezuka, Osamu**
***Adolf: A Tale of the Twentieth Century***
**Viz Media, 1996**
**ISBN 1569310580**
**$16.95**
**A**

*Adolf* is a historical novel told in five volumes, and incorporates a timeline into the narrative; this volume is the first. It is the story of three people named Adolf at the time of World War II: the infamous dictator; a half-Aryan/half-Japanese man; and a Jew living in Japan (and who is befriended by the half-Aryan prior to the war). The interplay of these three Adolfs gives Tezuka, one of the original practitioners of Japanese manga, an opportunity to examine the problems of racism, facism, and personal identity. The translation is a bit rocky, and the art may be too cartoony for some readers, but this final work from the *Astro Boy* animator is the closest to an epic in comics format since Spiegelman's *Maus.* The other titles include (in order) *An Exile in Japan, The Half-Aryan, Days of Infamy,* and 1945 and *All That Remains.*

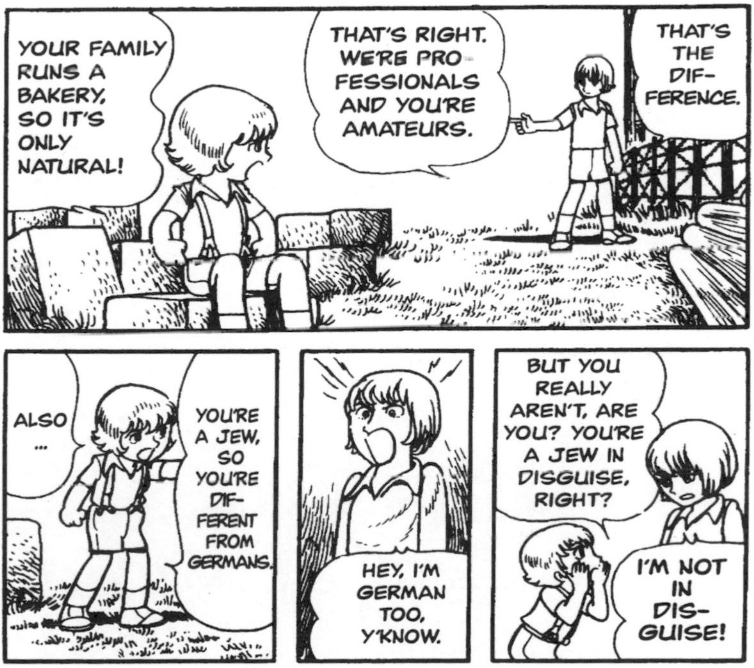
YOUR FAMILY RUNS A BAKERY, SO IT'S ONLY NATURAL!
THAT'S RIGHT. WE'RE PROFESSIONALS AND YOU'RE AMATEURS.
THAT'S THE DIFFERENCE.
ALSO ...
YOU'RE A JEW, SO YOU'RE DIFFERENT FROM GERMANS.
HEY, I'M GERMAN TOO, Y'KNOW.
BUT YOU REALLY AREN'T, ARE YOU? YOU'RE A JEW IN DISGUISE, RIGHT?
I'M NOT IN DISGUISE!

BUDDHA

**Tezuka, Osamu**
***Buddha Volume 1: Kapilavastu***
**Vertical Inc., 2003**
**ISBN 1932234438**
**$24.95**
**Y+**

In *Buddha,* a fictionalized life of the religious leader in eight volumes, Tezuka interprets the young man's life in a manner similar to Herman Hesse's prose novel, *Siddharta.* The cartooning style moves inside the reader's head as well as across the page. Other volumes in the series: *The Four Encounters, Devadatta, The Forest of Uruvela, Deer Park, Ananda, Prince Ajatasattu,* and *Jetavana.*

Blankets
CRAIG THOMPSON

**Thompson, Craig**
***Blankets: An Illustrated Novel***
**Top Shelf Productions, 2005**
**ISBN 1891830430**
**$29.95**
**Y+**

Thompson's first book, *Goodbye Chunky Rice,* was a cult hit, but *Blankets* is a breakout book detailing his experiences growing up in a fundamentalist Christian household. Thompson is in complete command of his material, and his illustration style is deft, unsentimental, and affecting. Weighing in at just under six hundred pages, this book may be the longest American graphic novel originally published in one volume.

Excuse me, but you look LOST.
...
I'm NOT.

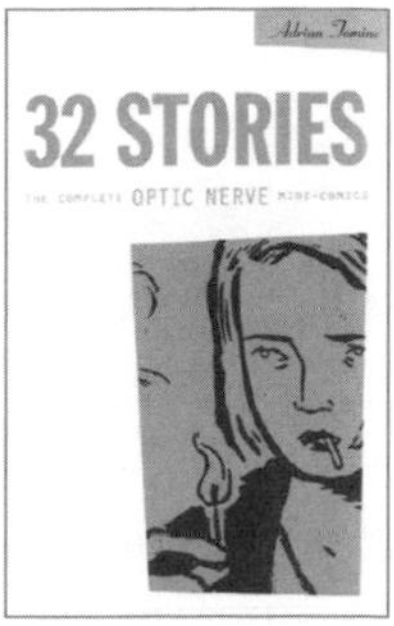
Adrian Tomine
32 STORIES
THE COMPLETE OPTIC NERVE MINI-COMICS

**Tomine, Adrian**
***32 Stories: The Complete Optic Nerve Mini-Comics***
**Drawn & Quarterly, 1998**
**ISBN 1896597009**
**$12.95**
**A**

Tomine is a photographer, capturing his subjects at their most revealing. These stories turn on the glance a character makes through a window blind, upon the knowledge that one is alone in the world, and other quiet and powerful understandings. Many of the stories have an autobiographical twist. Tomine has been compared to short story writer Raymond Carver, and that's accurate up to a point, but Tomine is more surrealistic in his conclusions.

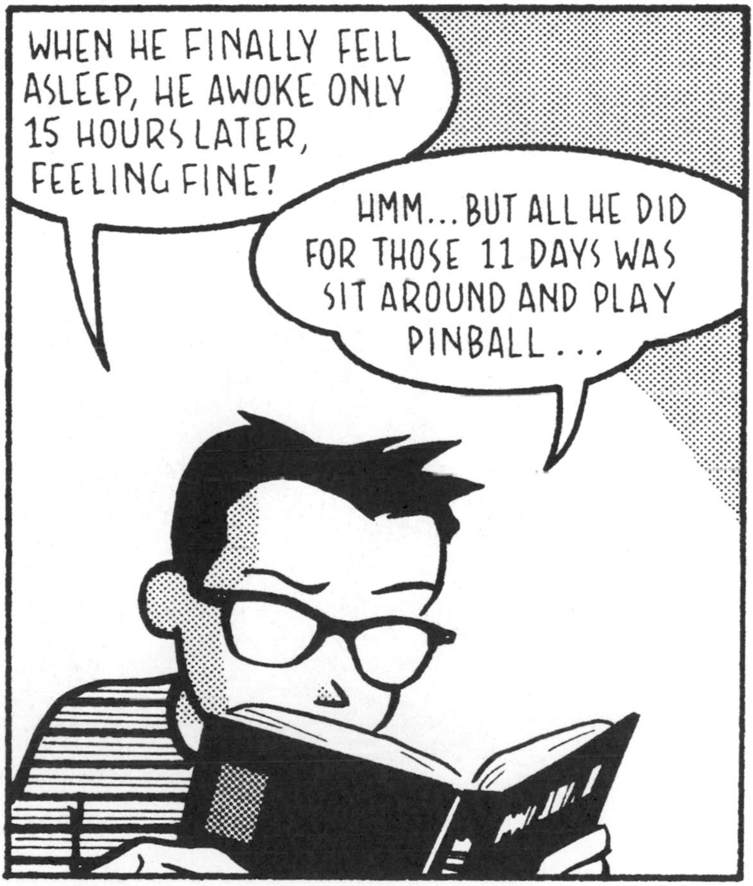
WHEN HE FINALLY FELL ASLEEP, HE AWOKE ONLY 15 HOURS LATER, FEELING FINE!
HMM... BUT ALL HE DID FOR THOSE 11 DAYS WAS SIT AROUND AND PLAY PINBALL...

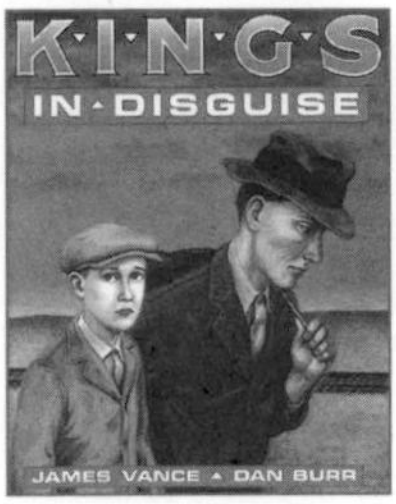
K·I·N·G·S
IN·DISGUISE
JAMES VANCE · DAN BURR

**Vance, James & Dan Burr**
***Kings in Disguise***
**W. W. Norton, 2005**
**ISBN 0393328481**
**$17.95**
**Y**

Set during the great depression, this book chronicles Freddie Bloch's search for his missing father. Possessing both lyracism and an oral depth, this excellent addition to the literature of the homeless comes close to a prose novel in its subtlety.

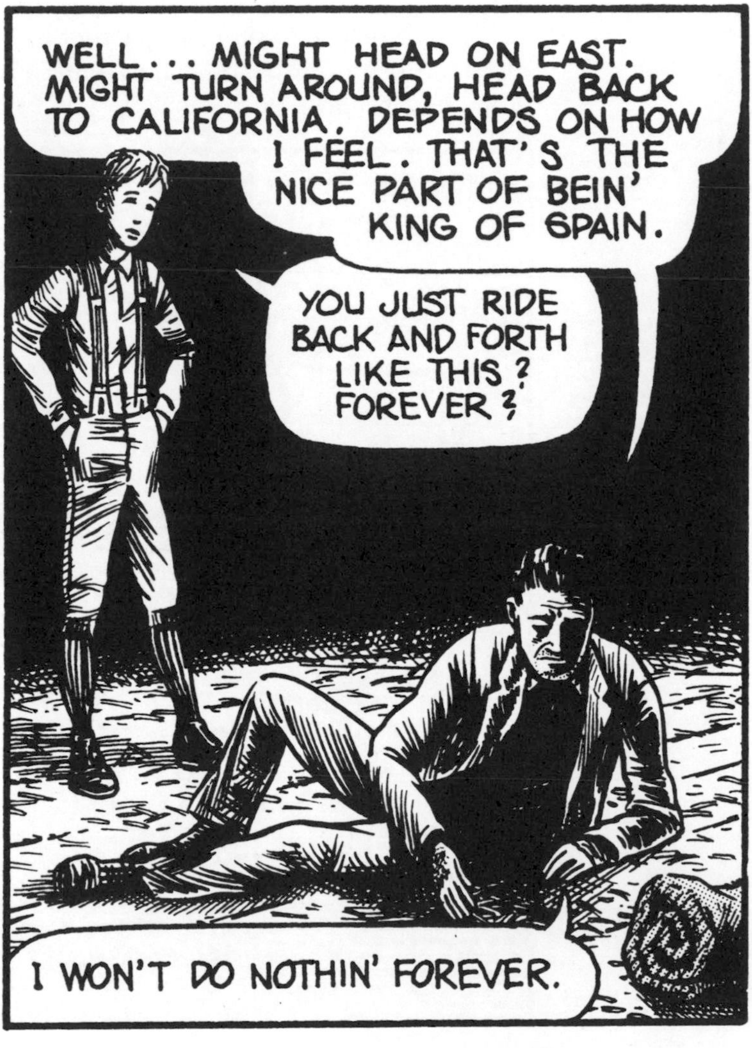
WELL... MIGHT HEAD ON EAST. MIGHT TURN AROUND, HEAD BACK TO CALIFORNIA. DEPENDS ON HOW I FEEL. THAT'S THE NICE PART OF BEIN' KING OF SPAIN.
YOU JUST RIDE BACK AND FORTH LIKE THIS? FOREVER?
I WON'T DO NOTHIN' FOREVER.

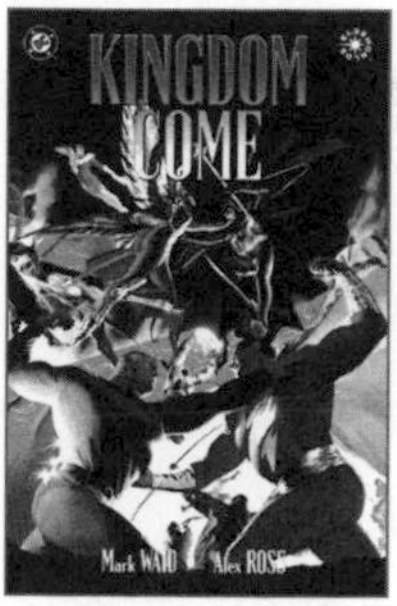
KINGDOM COME
Mark WAID
Alex ROSS

**Waid, Mark & Alex Ross**
***Kingdom Come***
**DC Comics, 1997**
**ISBN 1563893304**
**$14.95**
**Y**

This story begins ten years after Superman has entered into a self-imposed exile. All the old heroes such as Batman and Green Lantern have either vanished or are working covertly. Superman is called back into action because the new generation of superheroes have rejected the way of life that he upholds. The resolution is unexpected and startling, and includes the birth of the next generation of heroes.

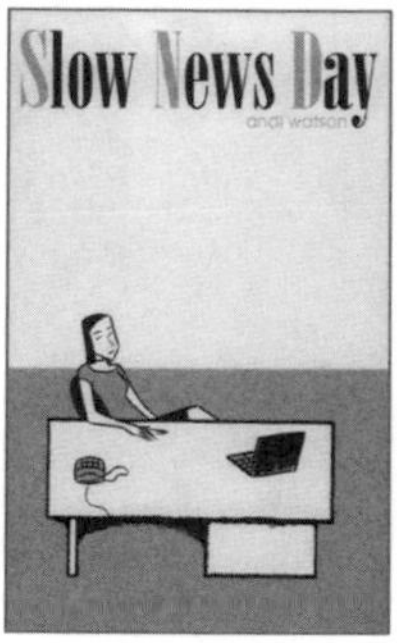
Slow News Day
andi watson

**Watson, Andi**
***Slow News Day***
**Slave Labor Graphics, 2002**
**ISBN 0943151597**
**$16.95**
**Y**

Katherine, an American with writing aspirations performing an internship at a small-town British newspaper, is at odds with Owen, an overly serious, cranky journalist who sees competition in Katherine and the new regime which seems more intent on delivering ads than news. As Owen and Katherine grow closer, Katherine begins to question her values and whether or not she wants a life in the fast lane. Watson breathes new life into the well-worn office romance-comedy with wit, unpredictability and simple, unpretentious drawings. *Slow News Day* is the equivalent of old Cary Grant comedies, entertaining with a touch of class.

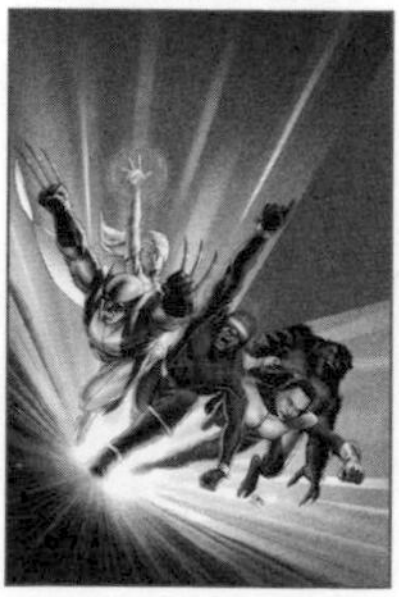

**Whedon, Joss & John Cassaday**
***Astonishing X-Men Volume 1: Gifted***
**Marvel Entertainment Group, 2004**
**ISBN 0785115315**
**$14.99**
**C**

The monthly *Astonishing X-Men* comic combines the most

popular superhero team in the world with the talents of Whedon, the creator of *Buffy the Vampire Slayer* and *Angel.* Whedon's penchant for snappy characterization is a perfect match for the high-adventure tales of the X-Men, and Cassaday's art is crisp and excellent. A second volume, entitled *Dangerous,* is also available.

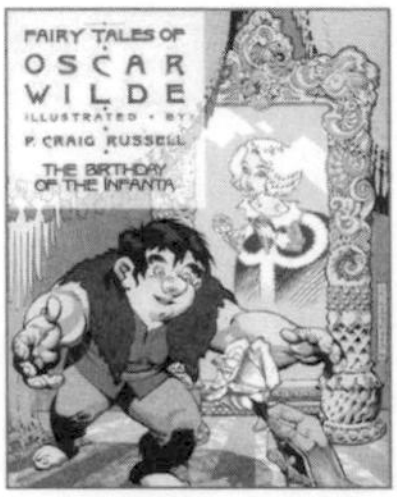
FAIRY TALES OF
OSCAR
WILDE
ILLUSTRATED • BY
P. CRAIG RUSSELL
THE BIRTHDAY OF THE INFANTA

**Wilde, Oscar & P. Craig Russell**
***The Fairy Tales of Oscar Wilde: The Birthday of the Infanta***
**NBM, 1998**
**ISBN 1561632139**
**$15.95**
**C**

This is one of a series of adaptations of Wilde's stories, which is handsomely presented and preserves the mythic quality of the tales by utilizing a colorful cartoon format. Other titles include *The Selfish Giant and the Star Child* and *The Young King and the Remarkable Rocket.*

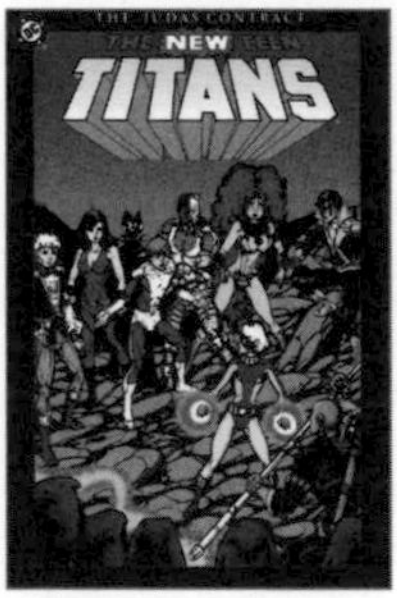
NEW
TITANS

**Wolfman, Marv & George Pérez**
***The New Teen Titans: The Judas Contract***
**DC Comics, 1991**
**ISBN 093028934X**
**$19.99**
**C**

In this stellar Teen Titans story many changes take place: Wally West gives up being Kid Flash, Dick Grayson retires his Robin identity in favor of being "Nightwing," an adult hero rather than a teen, and the Titans are betrayed by a heroine whom they've taken into their midst in one of the very best examples of the superhero mythos before it was rejuvenated by the vigilante hero concept of the late 1980s.

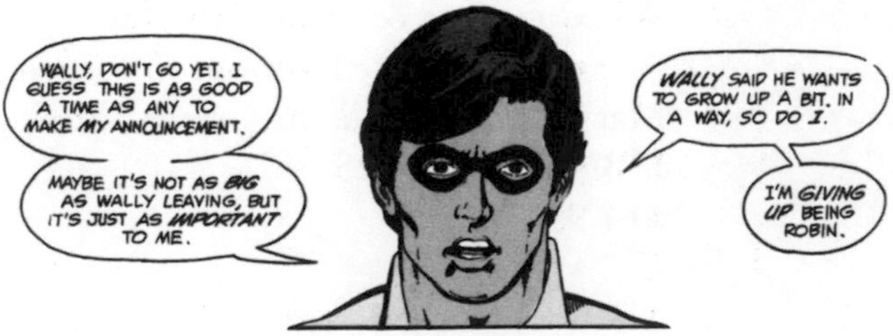
WALLY, DON'T GO YET. I GUESS THIS IS AS GOOD A TIME AS ANY TO MAKE MY ANNOUNCEMENT.
MAYBE IT'S NOT AS BIG AS WALLY LEAVING, BUT IT'S JUST AS IMPORTANT TO ME.
WALLY SAID HE WANTS TO GROW UP A BIT. IN A WAY, SO DO I.
I'M GIVING UP BEING ROBIN.

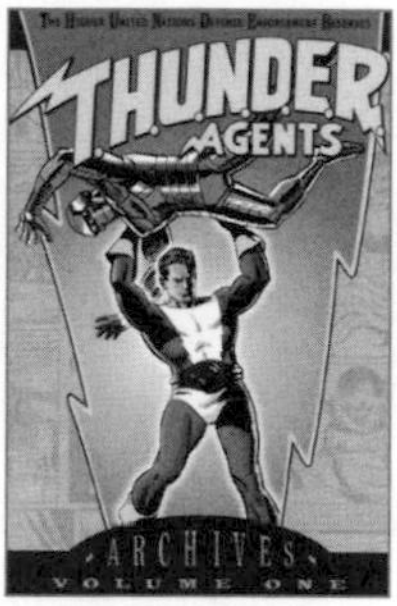
THUNDER
AGENTS
ARCHIVES
VOLUME ONE

**Wood, Wally**
***T.H.U.N.D.E.R. Agents Archives***
**DC Comics, 2002**
**ISBN 1563899035**
**$49.95**
**C**

Originally published in the 1960s, these stories combine the human problems in the superhero comic book popularized by Marvel Comics, the tight plotting utilized by DC Comics, and throws a bit of the espionage craze popular at the time into the mix. The "Archive" series published by DC Comics brings old comics back into print in a durable, well produced format. Other characters whose stories have been collected into the "Archive" format are Batman, Superman, Wonder Woman, and others.

# Further Reading!

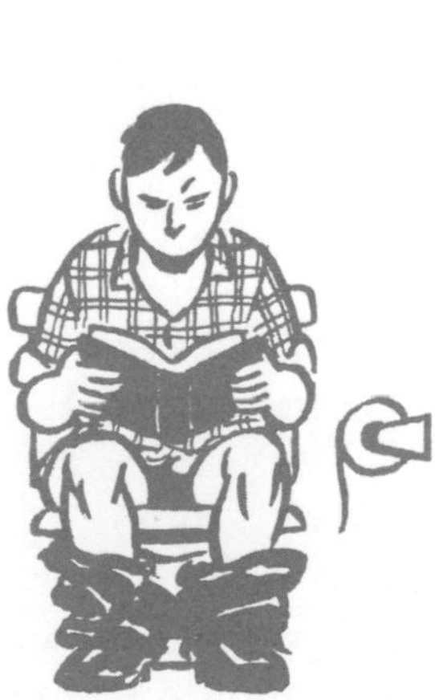

**Carey, Peter**
*Wrong about Japan: A Father's Journey with his Son*
**Alfred A Knopf, 2004**
**ISBN 1400043115 • $17.95**
In an attempt to better understand his shy son Charlie, novelist Carey (*My Life as a Fake, True History of the Kelley Gang*) follows his interest in manga, at first into comic-book specialty shops, which turns into an assignment: to go to Japan and interview the great anime and manga creators. Abundantly illustrated, *Wrong about Japan* is both a journey into parenthood and the manga craze.

**Chabon, Michael**
*The Amazing Adventures of Kavalier & Clay*
**Random House, 2000**
**ISBN 0312282990 • $15.00**
Chabon's novel, set during the early days of the comic-book industry, tells the story of immigrant cousins Joe Kavaliar and Sammy Clay, both modeled on early comic book creators. In the novel, Kavaliar and Clay create a hit character, the Escapist. Wrapped inside in this story of unrequited love and repressed lives, Chabon retells the story of the Senate investigation of the 1950s, and the creation of the Comics Code Authority. Awarded the Pulitzer Prize, Kavaliar & Clay is the most important novel ever written about the comic-book industry.

**Crumb, Robert**
*Your Vigor for Life Appalls Me:*
*Robert Crumb Letters 1958-1977*
**Fantagraphics Books, 1998**
**ISBN 1560973102 • $14.95**
In these letters, underground comix master Crumb reveals his search for meaning through thought, art, and sex. Includes some black and white illustrations in the form of letters.

**Daniels, Les**
*Marvel: Five Fabulous Decades*
*of the World's Greatest Comics*
**Abrams, 1993**
**ISBN 0810925664 • $26.95**
This single volume offers a concise and critical history of Marvel's rise to the forefront of the world of commercial comic book publishing. Includes biographical information on comic book creators as well as Marvel's famed

characters. Daniels has also written three similarly-themed volumes on the "big three" of DC Comics superhero-dom: *Batman, the Complete History: The Life and Times of the Dark Knight, Superman, the Complete History: The Golden Age of America's First Hero,* and *Wonder Woman, the Complete History: The Life and Times of the Amazon Princess.*

**Eisner, Will**
*Comics and Sequential Art*
**Poorhouse Press, 1985**
**ISBN 0961472812 • $22.99**
Comics grandmaster Eisner draws upon a career of creating and packaging comics and graphic novels, as well as a career as adjunct faculty at the School of Visual Arts, as he explains and demonstrates how sequential art is produced and why its effect is so powerful. Fully illustrated in black and white. The author includes numerous historical and international examples.

**Eisner, Will and Frank Miller, with Charles Brownstein**
*Eisner/Miller: One on One*
**Dark Horse, 2005**
**ISBN 1569717559 • $19.95**
Two of the most influential cartoonists in American history interview each other in this well illustrated, fascinating look at comics history, technical issues, working conditions, creativity, artistic integrity, and work habits.

**Feiffer, Jules**
*The Great Comic Book Heroes*
**Fantagraphics Books, 2003**
**ISBN 1560975016 • $8.95**
In 1964, Dial Press commissioned Feiffer to write a book on comic books as a nostalgic fad. In part a memoir, part social commentary, and part history, the original book included reproductions of early comic books. The new edition is limited to the essay in which Feiffer wards off McCarthyism and declares that junk culture serves a purpose.

**Gravett, Paul**
*Manga: Sixty Years of Japanese Comics*
**HarperCollins Design International, 2004**
**ISBN 1856693910 • $24.95**
Journalist and lecturer Gravett offers an informative and entertaining history

of Japanese comics and comics culture. He identifies themes in early manga, offers brief biographies of prominent creators, talks about how the market expanded to include girls' interests, and discusses the manga phenomenon, which started in Japan, but has grown to international proportions. This easy-to-read history is abundantly illustrated. If American readers recognize old film cartoons in these pictures that may be because the early manga masters studied American cartoons while learning to ply their trade.

**Horn, Maurice**
*The World Encyclopedia of Comics* (7 volumes)
**Chelsea House, 1998**
**ISBN 0791048543 • $35.00**
This update of the Horn classic from 1976 details characters, creators, and comics issues internationally. A vital addition to any comics library.

**Inge, M. Thomas**
*Charles M. Schulz: Conversations*
**University Press of Mississippi, 2000**
**ISBN 1578063051 • $20.00**
Noted comics historian Inge has edited a comprehensive volume of interviews with the late creator of *Peanuts*. Based on interviews conducted over a thirty-two-year period, this volume delves into the mind of arguably the greatest comic strip artist in American history. A biographical timeline of Schulz's life and illustrations are also included.

**Jones, Gerard**
*Men of Tomorrow: Geeks, Gangsters,*
*and the Birth of the Comic Book*
**Basic Books, 2004**
**ISBN 0465036570**
**$15.00**
Jones, a comic-book writer and the author of a few comic-book histories, vividly brings to life the creation of the American comic book in the 1930s, which evolved out of the science fiction movement of the 1920s, and landed squarely in the middle of popular culture with the first Superman story in 1938. Jones seasons the book with biographies of the major players—mostly Jews with a creative bent and few places to turn. The book also traces the evolution of Jerry Siegel and Joe Shuster's ultimately successful battle for recognition as the creators of Superman, one of the most enduring characters of twentieth-century popular culture.

**Jones, Gerard & Will Jacobs**
*The Comic Book Heroes*
**Prima Publishing, 1997**
**ISBN 0761503935 • $19.95**
Jones and Jacobs ably offer an history of the comics industry since the 1960s. Filled with insightful and up-to-date information, readers are given an overview of the field and clarity as to many of the challenges the industry faces. This book is a good companion to the excellent out-of-print history *The Steranko History of Comics* by Jim Steranko (Supergraphics, 1970).

**Juno, Andrea**
*Dangerous Drawings: Interviews with*
*Comix and Graphix Artists*
**Juno Books, 1997**
**ISBN 0965104281 • $24.95**
This book tries to present the viewpoint of the "underground" cartoonists, and includes interviews with Art Spiegelman, Dan Clowes, Julie Doucet, Chris Ware, Phoebe Glockner, and others.

**McCloud, Scott**
*Understanding Comics*
**HarperPerennial, 1994**
**ISBN 006097625X • $22.95**
McCloud's study is both a treatise on how comics work and a history of the medium. Its unique in the sense that it uses the comics medium to talk about itself, thus giving those evaluating and discussing the medium a common language. This is one of the best received books using comic format outside of the primarily comics' readership, and is a necessary volume on the language of the medium. Also recommended is McCloud's follow-up volume, *Reinventing Comics.*

**Moore, Alan**
*Alan Moore's Writing for Comics*
**Avatar Press, 2003**
**ISBN 1592910122 • $5.95**
One of the most creative forces in the history of mainstream comics whose credits include *Swamp Thing, Watchmen, League of Extraordinary Gentlemen,* and *V for Vendetta,* this book features Moore's theories on craft, and presents interesting and insightful aspects of comic-book writing.

**Robbins, Trina**
*A Century of Women Cartoonists*
**Kitchen Sink Press, 1993**
**ISBN 0878162003 • $16.95**
Unlocking a previously barred closet in comic book history, this book focuses on comic strips and comic books created, written, and drawn by women. Illustrated with numerous black-and-white examples.

**Rosenkranz, Patrick**
*Rebel Visions: The Underground*
*Comix Revolution 1963-1975*
**Fantagraphics Books, 2003**
**ISBN 1560974648 • $39.95**
The "underground comix" were first conceived amidst the hippie revolution in the 1960s, and popularized by R. Crumb's *Zap!* in 1968. This well-produced, heavily illustrated book traces the history of the underground movement and highlights prominent creators.

**Schreiner, Dave**
*Kitchen Sink Press: The First 25 Years*
**Kitchen Sink Press, 1994**
**ISBN 0878163077 • $25.00**
This history chronicles both the history of the now-defunct Kitchen Sink Press, one of the oldest independent comic book publishing houses in the United States, and in doing so, offers information on underground comics otherwise difficult to obtain. Including commentaries from creators and comics industry personnel, this book argues that comics, like any art, direct and reflect the culture out of which the art is created.

**Witek, Joseph**
*Comic Books as History: The Narrative Art of*
*Jack Jackson, Art Spiegelman, and Harvey Pekar*
**University of Mississippi Press, 1990**
**ISBN 0878054057 • $15.95**
Witek uses critical methodology as he examines the work of current comic artists from a critical perspective. This is a particularly useful work as it includes a lengthy study of Spiegelman's *Maus*.

# Title Index

*32 Stories: The Complete Optic Nerve Mini-Comics*—47
*300*—28

*Adolf: A Tale of the 20th Century*—45
*Age of Bronze: A Thousand Ships*—40
*Akira*—34
*Alia's Mission: Saving the Books of Iraq*—42
*Astonishing X-Men Volume 1: Gifted*—49
*Astro City*—SEE: *Kurt Busiek's Astro City*

*Barefoot Gen: A Cartoon History of Hiroshima*—32
*Batman: The Dark Knight Returns*—29
*Batman: Year One*—29
*Beowulf*—SEE: *The Collected Beowulf*
*Berlin Book 1: City of Stones*—26
*Blankets: An Illustrated Novel*—46
*Blood Song: A Silent Ballad*—13
*The Bloody Streets of Paris*—44
*The Blue Witch of Oz*—40
*Bone: Out from Boneville*—41
*The Books of Magic*—15
*The Borden Tragedy: A Memoir of the Infamous Double Murder at Fall River, Mass., 1892*—17
*Buddha Volume 1: Kapilavatsu*—46

*Cages*—27
*The Cartoon History of the Universe*—SEE: *Larry Gonick's The Cartoon History of the Universe*
*Catwoman: Selina's Big Score*—11
*City of Glass*—5
*City of Light, City of Dark: A Comic Book Novel*—5
*Classic Star Wars*—18
*Clumsy*—9
*Clyde Fans Book 1*—38
*The Collected Beowulf*—21
*The Complete Crumb Comics Volume 15: Featuring Modele Oday and Her Pals*—12
*A Contract with God Trilogy*—13

*Daredevil: Born Again*—30

## Title Index

*A Distant Soil: The Gathering*—12

*ElfQuest: Archives Volume 1*—35
*ElfQuest: Wolfrider Volume 1*—35
*Epileptic*—6
*The Essential Avengers Volume 1*—25
*The Essential Fantastic Four Volume 1*—25
*The Essential Spider-Man Volume 1*—25

*The Fairy Tales of Oscar Wilde: The Birthday of the Infanta*—50
*From Hell*—31

*Ghost in the Shell*—40
*Ghost World*—11
*Give It Up! and Other Stories by Franz Kafka*—22
*The Golem's Mighty Swing*—43
*The Grasshopper and the Ant*—25
*The Greatest Joker Stories Ever Told*—19
*The Greatest Superman Stories Ever Told*—19
*The Greatest Team-Up Stories Ever Told*—19
*Green Lantern/Green Arrow Volume 2*—33
*Guilty*—43

*Hellboy: Seed of Destruction*—27
*Hey Buddy!: Volume 1 of the Complete Buddy Bradley Stories from Hate*—6
*Hikaru No Go*—21

*I Never Liked You*—9
*It's a Good Life if You Don't Weaken*—39

*Jack the Ripper: A Journal of the Whitechapel Murders, 1888-1889*—17
*A Jew in Communist Prague Volume 1: Loss of Innocence*—17

*King: A Comics Biography of Martin Luther King Jr.*—5
*Kingdom Come*—49
*Kings in Disguise*—48
*Kurt Busiek's Astro City: Life in the Big City*—10

*Larry Gonick's The Cartoon History of the Universe*—18

*Leave it to Chance Volume 1: Shaman's Rain*—36
*Lone Wolf and Cub: The Assassin's Road*—24

*Mai the Psychic Girl: The Perfect Collection*—24
*Marvels*—11
*Maus: A Survivor's Tale*—42
*The Metamorphosis*—22
*Mr. Punch*—16
*Mother Come Home*—21

*Nancy Drew: The Demon of River Heights*—35
*The New Teen Titans: The Judas Contract*—50

*Oh My Goddess: Wrong Number*—15
*Optic Nerve*—SEE: *32 Stories: The Complete Optic Nerve Mini-Comics*
*Our Cancer Year*—8
*Owly Volume 1: The Way Home & The Bittersweet Summer*—36

*Palestine*—37
*Palomar: The Heartbreak Soup Stories*—20
*Paul Has a Summer Job*—36
*Persepolis: The Story of a Childhood*—38

*The Saga of the Swamp Thing*—30
*Salmon Doubts*—37
*Same Difference and Other Stories*—22
*Samurai Executioner: When the Demon Knife Weeps*—24
*The Sandman: The Doll's House*—15
*Sin City: The Hard Goodbye*—28
*Slow News Day*—49
*A Small Killing*—31
*The Spirit Archives Volume 1*—14
*Star Wars*—SEE: *Classic Star Wars*
*Strangers in Paradise: I Dream of You*—32
*Suspended in Language: Neils Bohr's Life, Discoveries, and the Century He Shaped*—34
*Swamp Thing: Dark Genesis*—30

*The Tale of One Bad Rat*—44
*Tantrum!*—14

# Title Index

*T.H.U.N.D.E.R. Agents Archives*—51
*Trigun Volume 1*—33

*The Ultimate Spider-Man: Power and Responsibility*—8
*Usagi Yojimbo Book 1: The Ronin*—38

*Violent Cases*—16

*Walt Disney's Uncle Scrooge: The Mines of King Solomon*—8
*Watchmen*—31
*Why I Hate Saturn*—7

*Yu-Gi-Oh! Volume 1*—44

*X-Men*—SEE: *Astonishing X-Men Volume 1: Gifted*

# Other books by Stephen Weiner

---

*The Will Eisner Companion*
with N.C. Christopher Couch

*Faster Than a Speeding Bullet: The Rise of the Graphic Novel*

*100 Graphic Novels for Public Libraries*

*Bring an Author to Your Library*

---

NBM has over 200 graphic novels from America and Europe available.
Ask for our complete color catalog:
NBM Publishing
555 8th Avenue, Suite 1202
New York, NY 10018

Visit our Web site to view our complete catalog and order any of our publications.
Librarians: visit our Library page at our Web site for recommendations
www.nbmpublishing.com

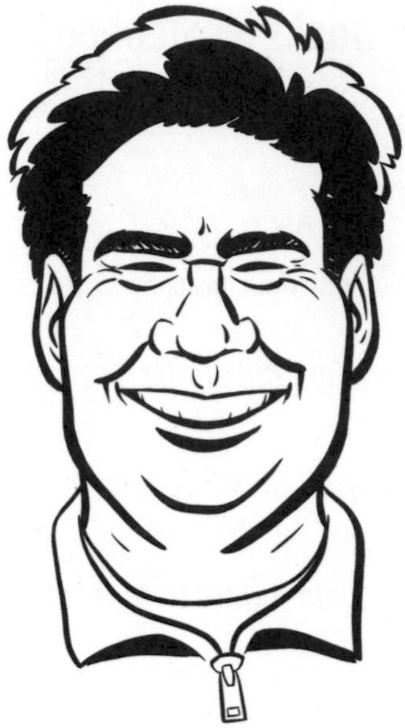

**Stephen Weiner** is the director of the Maynard Public Library in Maynard, Massachusetts, and is a comics historian and critic who has been a pioneering advocate for the inclusion of graphic novels in public libraries and educational settings. He holds an MA degree in Children's Literature as well as an MLIS. He has been writing about comic art since 1992, and has published articles and reviews in *Voice of Youth Advocates, The Comics Buyer's Guide, Diamond Dialogue, School Library Journal, Library Journal, The Children's Book Council Newsletter, Comic Book Artist, The Shy Librarian, Brodart Graphic Novels Newsletter, Graphic Novel Review, Bookmarks,* and *The English Journal.* His books include: *Bring an Author to Your Library* (The Highsmith Press, 1993), *100 Graphic Novels for Public Libraries* (Kitchen Sink Press, 1996), *The 101 Best Graphic Novels* (NBM, 2001), and *Faster than a Speeding Bullet: The Rise of the Graphic Novel* (NBM, 2003). In addition, he is co-author (with N.C. Christopher Couch) of *The Will Eisner Companion* (DC Comics, 2004).

**Keith R.A. DeCandido** has been, at various times, a best-selling author, book editor, anthologist, comics writer, critic, and TV personality in the comics, science fiction, fantasy, and horror fields. He is the author of two seminal articles on comics in libraries in *Library Journal* in the early 1990s, and has written articles and reviews on comics for *LJ, Publishers Weekly, The Comics Journal, Creem, Wilson Library Bulletin,* and SFRevu.com. He is the editor of many acclaimed anthologies, most recently *Star Trek: Tales from the Captain's Table,* as well as 2003's *Imaginings: An Anthology of Long Short Fiction,* one story from which was nominated for a Nebula Award. Find out more about Keith at his web site, www.DeCandido.net.

Illustration by Chris Shadoian